Telling Tales

Storytelling as Emotional Literacy

Written by:

TAFFY THOMAS and STEVE KILLICK

First published
September 07 in Great Britain by

PUBLISHING

© Taffy Thomas/Steve Killick 2007

The moral right of the authors has been asserted in accordance with the
Copyright, Designs and Patents Act 1988

ISBN-10: 1-905637-28-4
ISBN-13: 978-1-905637-28-7

Educational Printing Services Limited
Albion Mill, Water Street, Great Harwood, Blackburn BB6 7QR
Telephone: (01254) 882080   Fax: (01254) 882010
E-mail: enquiries@eprint.co.uk   Website: www.eprint.co.uk

Acknowledgements

To Sarah, Ciara, Seamus, Chrissy, Rosie, Sam and Aimee who have had to live with our attempts at emotional literacy.

Thanks also to Dominic Kelly, Neil Frude, Mark Rivett and Dick Berry for their invaluable assistance.

Three Golden Apples fell from the sky

The first is for you, who told the story.

The second is for you, who listened to it.

The third I take in my right hand, and toss it over my left shoulder

for all the people who told the stories before me.

When you tell a story, the ghosts of all those who told it before stand behind you - they are there to help you.

Taffy Thomas

Taffy Thomas trained as a Literature and Drama teacher at Dudley College of Education. He then taught for several years in Wolverhampton. He founded and directed the legendary folk theatre company, Magic Lantern, travelling Europe illustrating folk songs with shadow puppets and much more! He founded and directed the rural community arts company, Charivari, with their popular touring unit, the Fabulous Salami Brothers, which he fronted and performed in, until a stroke at the age of 36 sidelined him. He turned back to story telling as self-imposed speech therapy.

Taffy has a repertoire of more than 300 stories, tales and elaborate lies collected mainly from traditional oral sources, which he is happy to tell in almost any situation. He is now the most experienced English storyteller having pioneered many storytelling residencies and appeared at the National Storytelling Festival in the USA and the Bergen Arts Festival in Norway. In 2001 Taffy performed new collaboration for the Blue Peter Prom at the Royal Albert Hall. In 2006 he was storyteller in residence for the programme of summer residencies at the National Centre for Storytelling in Jonesborough, Tennessee.

He is currently artistic director of Tales in Trust, the Northern Centre for Storytelling, in Grasmere, the Lake District. In the 2001 New Year Honours List he was awarded the MBE for services to storytelling and charity. He tours nationally and internationally working in both entertainment and education and is also a patron of the Society for Storytelling.

Steve Killick

Dr Steve Killick is a Consultant Clinical Psychologist working in the NHS in South Wales with young people with severe emotional and mental health problems. He has worked in both adult and child education and health settings and is Consultant Psychology Advisor to NCH Schools. He is Honorary Senior Tutor for the School of Psychology at Cardiff University and co-founder of FACETS Psychology Consultancy.

As well as published papers, he has written 'Giving Sorrow Words - Managing Bereavement in Schools' and 'Emotional Literacy at the Heart of the School Ethos'. He has also written and produced several training films in the areas of child development and mental health.

Steve has a long interest in storytelling and has performed and taught in this area as well as using storytelling in his work. He is currently performing a storytelling show based on the stories of the Brothers Grimm.

Contents

Introduction

This book is for teachers, learning support assistants, mentors, indeed all those who work with children and young people in schools or elsewhere. It is about the positive influence that telling a story, as opposed to reading, can have on a child's learning, particularly in the domains of social and emotional learning. It is a process of speaking and listening that creates a powerful educational methodology. As education becomes more focused on new technologies and media, an activity that requires nothing more than the 'presence of minds' has a lot to offer.

Storytelling is, at its best, an art form and one in which everyone can develop skills. This universal form of expression is based in the safe relationship between teller and listener. Stories speak of our desires, dreams and anxieties and can inspire our imagination. So, storytelling is a bridge between the inner psychological world and the outer real world. As such it is particularly useful in helping develop social and emotional skills in children and that is the central premise of this book – storytelling can build emotional literacy. This process begins with listening to stories and can be developed as children gain the confidence to tell and create their own stories. In so doing, they have a valuable tool to shape their experience. Before they can begin to write a story, children need to imagine it, and to tell it!

By being able to confidently tell stories with emotional depth and resonance, teachers have a valuable tool to engage children in the learning process. Projects such as T3 (Teachers Telling Tales) in Northern Ireland aim to reintroduce this timeless pedagogic tool back into education settings by giving teachers the chance to learn storytelling skills from professional storytellers. There is a resurgence of interest in the oral tradition of telling stories. This book aims to give adults working with children the confidence and resources to tell stories to children and young people. At this time the engagement of young people in education has never been more important. Storytelling can help with this, in all areas of the curriculum, but perhaps most by building well-being and community.

Telling stories is a skilful occupation but we all have the potential of finding a way of using this method of communication. It is an essentially democratic activity that can involve all. As one person tells a story another wants to respond, they naturally lead to sharing. Storytelling is reciprocal in nature and can contribute to calmer classrooms, confident children and safer schools.

In **Part One** of the book, Steve gives a theoretical basis to using stories and storytelling to develop social and emotional aspects of learning. Chapter 1 gives a broad sweep across how stories help children learn and assist in psychological development. Chapter 2 outlines the principles underlying emotional literacy, a movement that emphasises the value and importance of understanding feelings in ourselves and others and its application in education. Chapter 3 weaves these ideas together and describes how storytelling can be used to enhance emotional literacy in schools.

Part Two is a 'How To' section. In Chapter 1 Taffy helps give the confidence and skills necessary to tell a story. Chapter 2 describes some methods to help children tell and create stories.

The final section, **Part Three**, consists of many traditional folk tales and stories that can be told in school or anywhere working with children.   Most of these stories come from Taffy's extensive collection. There is a wide variety of stories appealing across the age range that can be learnt to be told individually or in groups by teachers, parents, mentors or indeed anybody working with children or adults. Traditional stories are used not because they are the only kind of story to develop emotional and social growth but because they are entertaining, engaging, have emotional resonance and are a foundation for building the skills in using stories to promote emotional literacy. When you tell a story you give a gift, the listeners will take from it and use it as they will. This section also includes some appendices for further reading and useful organisations and resources.

Part One

1 - The Language of Imagination - How storytelling facilitates learning.

"Storytelling is one of the most important, most humane, most liberating and most democratic things that human beings can do, and it should have a central place in every classroom."

Philip Pullman

Stories and story-telling have been an integral part of what human beings have done with each other since we have learned the power of language. Stories have always been a powerful source of entertainment and education. They have been a way of conquering fears, realising dreams, sharing sadness, remembering the past and building hope for the future. Such tales are often told in communal or domestic settings where people come together to share the experience of the story. By this process, stories have helped to form how we see ourselves and have helped create a sense of identity. With new technologies and higher levels of literacy the form of communication that is narrative or story may seem outdated or even primitive. However, it remains one of the most powerful forms of communication and shows no sign of being forgotten as the interest generated through the storytelling revival shows.

Storytelling has always been an important part of the process of how we raise and educate children both formally in schools and informally through parenting or mentoring. However, the emphasis on literacy has often meant that a greater value has been put on reading stories to children with the intention that they learn to read for themselves. Although this is admirable it also loses the social process that takes place between the teller and listener that can do so much to engage and educate. This book explores how story telling can be used in many different ways to help children engage and learn in educational contexts, particularly in the realms of emotional and social development. Although primarily aimed at schools, there will be much that is directly relevant to all those who work with children in many different capacities.

The ultimate objective of using storytelling with children is to help them become good storytellers themselves – so that they are able to tell stories, full of the rich complexities of our emotional lives that tell of competence, compassion and optimism that reflects a belief in one's self. In a society where so many people find themselves isolated, disenfranchised and suspicious of others, such skills are necessary. In this book, ideas developed in the field of emotional literacy are used to give a framework in exploring how stories can be used to promote academic development, behaviour and co-operation and, perhaps most importantly, to build a sense of personal well-being and confidence that increases the motivation to learn.

How Stories Stimulate Learning

There has been a worldwide resurgence of interest in the importance of oral storytelling. This is the telling of stories, told from an active imagination not learnt word for word and includes traditional tales handed down for generations and more personal, family or community stories that give a sense of culture and tradition. Also, new stories created from the imagination can be brought to life this way. The primary reason for telling such stories is often that of entertainment, however, there is often much more to storytelling than just an exercise in distraction, important though that is. The importance of storytelling in several fields such as health, education, building and sustaining communities is being recognised or, perhaps, it may be better put as being rediscovered. It has been said that 'stories remind us of what we already know' and we are now being reminded of the value of storytelling.

Oral storytelling has a number of functions, all of which have implications for education. Understanding these functions helps the teacher, or others working in schools, to use stories as an educational tool. It is because storytelling works on so many levels that it is one of the most powerful methods we have in relating and communicating to others. The ideas given here are adapted from the work of Robin Gwyndaf about the purposes of oral storytelling (1).

The Functions of Storytelling

Entertainment

The fact that stories are entertaining is a clue to their enduring popularity. On a basic level they can distract us from other concerns and engage us in the story. We are drawn to know what happens next. That stories entertain and engage is key to understanding why they are so effective in the learning process. Our attention is given to them, which starts us thinking about the stories. There may also be messages in the story contained at a metaphorical level that also influences us. It is important that we are prepared to 'suspend disbelief' to listen to a story and that it has authenticity even if it is not factually true. When we hear stories we become engaged and our curiosity is awakened. This curiosity can be transferred into motivation for learning. Storytelling helps the relationship between teacher and learner. The class can become alive and students can experience that learning can be fun. We always remember the teacher who told us stories – it helps develop positive relationships. This may echo what for most people is the relationship in which they were first told stories, that of one with a caring parent. Hearing stories in a group is also a positive, shared experience. A tale can bring people together in a community. The capacity of stories to entertain and engage should not be underestimated in the learning process.

Informative

Stories tell us about the world and how people work. Stories, from those that we read about or see on TV or at the movies, through to personal anecdotes, give shape to our experience and tell us how the world works. There may seem to be an important distinction between stories that are 'true' and those that are 'false' but this distinction may not be clear-cut. The perception of truth is often a personal matter and what might matter more is that the story has some emotional 'truth' rather than being factually correct. Rather it may be that stories create narratives about the world, about power and whose story it is that is being told. It is important to be able to evaluate the content and meaning of stories one hears and to be able to develop new stories. We are told about the world in which we live through the stories we hear. This means that as well as being imaginative listeners we also need to be critical listeners. Such listeners do not believe everything they hear but are able to discriminate and find the meaning in the story.

Stories are also lies and can be used to deceive. They may invent and reinforce negative stereotypes particularly of race, religion and gender. Differences between people have always been amplified by stories often emphasising negative attributes of the other group. Gossip is often a way of telling negative stories of others in a way that cannot be answered. It might be argued that politicians and journalists are storytellers who place a 'spin' on a story so that it is perceived in a certain way. What might differentiate a storyteller from someone using stories to deceive is the openness of the fantasy world of story. It is an invitation to enter a world that is beyond the world of facts, beyond a simple definition of true and false. A storyteller takes an ethical position.

Stories are, of course, relevant to every subject. Storytelling is being seen increasingly as a vital tool in developing literacy. How can a child be expected to write a creative story if she at first can't tell it, or imagine it? For young people facing classical or modern texts, storytelling is a great way in. One teacher brought the works of Chaucer and Shakespeare alive by telling the stories orally before beginning to study it – the students became engaged in the action of the plot and were not left so mystified by the language. Science too can be helped through stories that tell of how inventions or discoveries were made. History is brought alive by stories of the past rather than by the clinical examination of facts. The word 'history' shares the same root as the word 'story' from the meaning of a narrative or relating of events. In fact, it is difficult to think of an area of education where using stories would not be relevant – they have even been used successfully in teaching maths and number skills as they help develop sequencing. Stories not only help engage the child in the subject but also, because of the power of the **narrative thread**, help the child remember. For all subjects, the curiosity engendered by the stories is then the springboard for wanting to find out more.

Stories are perfect tools for **imparting wisdom** in how to live and all cultures have a tradition of teaching tales. Stories such as the 'Boy who cried Wolf' or 'Solomon and the Baby' teach important social lessons. Many religions use stories to further wisdom and spiritual understanding. For helping young minds understand many subtle aspects of the human psyche such as how our desire to avoid looking stupid can lead us precisely to that destination, it would be hard to find a more effective way than to tell the story of the 'Emperor's New Suit', (see page 106). This story, recorded by Hans Christian Anderson, is an example of an old story passed on through the oral tradition for generations before it was ever written down.

When we hear a story we are invited to reflect on the actions of the characters in the story. We can learn from their cleverness or from their foolishness, we are able to reflect on decisions and consequences of behaviour. We can judge and evaluate the intentions and motivations of a character and decide if they are justified. We can learn from their dilemmas and choices, whether they are about the character of a real person living in our own world or a fictitious person in a story, set far, far away and a long time ago. This makes a story a very powerful teaching methodology, not least, because the wisdom in the story can instruct indirectly or through metaphor. Of course, what the listener hears may not be what the teller intends, but the meaning the listener constructs in response to the story is much more likely to be of use to that person.

Emotional Understanding

Stories are particularly useful at helping our emotional and social understanding, which makes them so useful in developing emotional literacy. Stories are a way of talking about our inner lives, our thoughts, feelings and motivations but they can do this without intruding into personal issues. Stories give us a way of being able to think about feelings that is critical for mental health and well-being. Stories also inform us about the universal nature and process of emotions. The fact that stories are able to help us learn about feelings and how to manage them is central to themes of this book. One of the reasons why stories are so important in this area is because it allows us to talk about what is most personal without intruding into the privacy of children's own inner lives. They make it possible to learn that many complex feelings we experience, positive feelings such as joy, love and excitement or more challenging and disturbing feelings such as shame, fear, or rejection, are not limited to our own experience but shared by others. We learn that what is most personal is most universal. Stories are the most natural way of helping children build and learn an emotional vocabulary. Margot Sunderland said *'everyday language is not the natural language of feeling for children. Their natural language is that of image and metaphor, as in stories and dreams'* (2).

The Transmission of Values and Morality

Stories are able to communicate powerful messages about what 'values' a culture or society holds to be important. Qualities seen as positive can be rewarded and those seen as negative can be punished. For instance, compassion, bravery, forgiveness or patience can be seen as virtues whose practice is often rewarded. This is not to say that stories should have an obvious 'moral' as that is often counter-productive. The listener is active in finding meaning in the story and will draw his or her own conclusions. The common conflict between 'good' and 'evil' is usually resolved in stories and in this resolution enables us to experience healing and validation in our own good choices and membership of a common group. In this sense stories are an important transmitter of social values and change. Jack Zipes said *"Storytelling has always had and still has two basic functions: first and foremost to communicate the relevant values, norms and customary practices of a group of people – to conserve them and pass them on to future generations so that they will be better able to survive. The second function is to question, change, and overthrow the dominant value system - to transform what has been preserved so that the values, norms and customs enable a group of people not only to survive but to improve their lives..."* (From Wilson, 2006, Note 3).

Stories and traditional stories in particular can communicate strong ideas about morality, about what is right and wrong about how we should treat ourselves and

6

others. They can also attack and be subversive to authority and comment on the misuse of power. We are all drawn to stories where good triumphs over evil reflecting our wishes and hopes for a just world. Values-based stories help children reflect on moral and social issues and traditional tales are particularly useful here. All cultures appear to have examples of these tales and there are many examples of these given in Part Three of this book. It is important to note that although these are 'moral tales' the moral is not made apparent by boldly stating at the end, 'the moral of the story is….'. This is to rob the listener of the opportunity of finding their own meaning in the story. People find their own meanings in stories and what they find is perhaps what will be most useful to them. Often, if a moral or learning point is too explicit it can leave the listener feeling disappointed or even manipulated. Ambiguity can be more effective.

Meaning, Identity and Community

When we listen to stories we are always in a process of projecting ourselves into and identifying with the story. They engage our natural curiosity about the world which can be encouraged in the classroom to create an attitude of questioning, why are things as they are? What things are and are not possible? These questions develop thinking skills particularly around the social and physical rules by which our world is governed, the world, who we are in it and where we are going. Stories also tell us about worlds different from our own, different families, organisations, communities and cultures either real or imagined. Storytelling can be a way of *building bridges across and within communities*' (4) and this can value diversity and combat prejudice. The work of storytelling groups around the world has often been concerned with the purposes of building communities and healing divisions through understanding given in stories. Stories are also vehicles for talking about our highest aspirations of love, compassion and justice. When a story is told, a community of listeners is instantly created. Many of the stories told today have been travelling around the world for thousands of years, being adapted to different settings and reflecting particular issues. Versions of 'Cinderella' have been traced back to Medieval China and Ancient Egypt. Despite differences and local adaptations, the stories may reflect basic human concerns and issues.

Speaking and Listening

A told tale needs a listener to hear it and the process of listening to stories builds listening skills. Listening to stories develops language skills not only in vocabulary but learning about the structure of language and these in turn develop expressive language skills. The listener becomes better able to tell stories, which demands skills of structuring beginning, middle and endings and relational skills of emotional authenticity or truthfulness. These skills of speaking and listening are powerful interpersonal and communication skills of discourse and presentation as well as having other benefits on development as discussed later.

Imaginative and Metaphorical Thinking

Storytelling uses language to **paint pictures** in the listener's minds. In this way it develops imaginative and visual thinking which are important components of creativity. This is useful for a wide range of subjects requiring creative skills. Children are much better able to write a creative story if they are able to tell a creative story, and storytelling builds the skills to be able to do this. Upon listening to a story well told, the listener imagines and visualises for themselves the pictures and images presented in the story. The 'image' is that seen in the imagination and although this is also true of reading stories, the storyteller has non-verbal skills of tone of voice, gesture and posture to fuel the listener's imagination. Storytelling might even be seen as a visual art more than a literary one. To develop this further, stories can bring 'vision' and inspiration. Stories, like language itself, are metaphors which help us to think about things in different ways. This can help problem solving skills develop and with inspiration comes motivation. Stories also speak to our dreams and it is no coincidence that a common time for storytelling or reading fiction is before going to sleep, the threshold of the dream world where our thoughts are ruled by metaphor and symbol (5). The human brain learns much from metaphor. It gives a way of being able to think about and understand something by relating it to something that is already known and to link concepts together. To be able to think metaphorically is clearly an important skill to develop. Metaphor can also communicate beyond conscious thought and send messages into the subconscious. Many stories have, at their core, a struggle between good and evil. Most often good transcends evil after overcoming some considerable obstacle and this ending is not only satisfying, it may also teach us important lessons about the world. The question is, of course, who determines what is 'good' and 'evil' in any story? Stories can also be used to manipulate, misinform and deceive. Integrity is essential.

Relationships

Stories are often concerned with how people get along, how they feel when in conflict and what they can do to sort things out. The teacher or parent telling a story to another is also in relation and can modulate the story depending on the reactions of the listeners. If a scary story is too upsetting for the listeners it can be softened to be more reassuring, stories can contain the emotion. If it isn't stimulating enough, the emotions can be intensified. As well as the emotional content, stories contain much about how to get along with others, what others might be thinking or planning, who might be trusted and who might not, how best to communicate with them and solve problems.

In telling stories, relationships are also built in the real world as well as the imaginative world. Storytelling is a very non-threatening activity and there is no component of failure in listening to a story – the child can feel safe and also valued. Many people have said that the teachers they remember most clearly, and most fondly, were the ones that told them stories.

Awareness of the Physical World

Many traditional stories involve the physical world. From creation myths, through to the deep dark forests of fairy tales, through to the many stories that involve animals. A focus on the natural world increases respect for it and fosters a valuing of the environment. At a time when awareness of the environment and the need to take care of it has never been more critical, stories can help engender in children a respect to take care of things and again stories can do this by direct example or through metaphor.

Stories can be linked to particular rituals that take place throughout the year in a way that marks the turning of the seasons. The Story of Bhride, an old Celtic story, is often remembered in Scotland, Wales and Ireland and told at Candlemas at the beginning of February to mark awareness of the imminent changing of the seasons. The darkness of winter will pass and spring will succeed. Particular stories are associated with times of the year, and seasonal rituals remind us of ancient traditions and our connection with the physical world.

The Influence of Storytelling on Child Development

Such is the power of bringing stories to life by telling that it should not be restricted only to young children who have not yet fully mastered reading. Stories are a powerful way of connecting to all, children, young people and adults. Professional storytellers are becoming more frequent visitors into schools, reflecting the growing recognition of the value of live and skilled storytelling. However, storytelling should not be seen as a specialised talent that only a few possess. Rather it is a vital communication skill in which we can all develop our own skills and ability regardless of age or ability. Feeling confident to tell stories, be it of our own everyday experiences or from other sources, helps us engage with others and storytelling is a reciprocal social activity. When one person tells a story it often reminds the listener of an experience that they wish to give an account of. Friendships and intimate relationships grow by reciprocal storytelling so these speaking and listening skills transfer and develop to other social skills as well. Good storytellers are often popular because of their skills in entertaining. While only some may become this socially valued, developing these skills in all young people will aid many aspects of their academic development and more. Storytelling contributes to many aspects of human development.

Stories, as means of communication, have existed for tens of thousands of years of human history. It should not be surprising that storytelling aids many aspects of human development particularly those linked to learning. The evidence for the role of stories and narrative in these strands of development varies and they are without doubt interconnected. Examining the impact of stories on these different aspects of development enables a consideration of how stories can assist the learning process.

- **Language** – listening to stories aids contextual learning of language. We learn language best when we hear it spoken in context and stories provide a context in which vocabulary and grammar is learnt. Exposure to the rich language of storytelling at a young age has a marked beneficial effect on the development of language and appreciation of literature (6) as listening to stories helps language development. Problems with language are often associated with behavioural problems and often children have difficulties in understanding the verbal and non-verbal cues in the communication of others. When someone is telling a story, such features are often exaggerated to help get the meaning across, through gesture or tone of voice. This exaggeration helps the child learn more about

STORY TYPES

We are surrounded by stories of all different types; journalists talk of news stories, there are stories in films, drama, soap operas, novels and literature. Also, we tell each other the everyday stories of our lives in gossip and anecdote. In the oral tradition there are many different types of story told and some categories are listed below – some stories would fit into several different categories.

Fairy tales – or traditional, folk or wonder tales

These stories are the backbone of the oral tradition, stories that were handed down through generations by word of mouth rather than written down. Although often known as fairy stories they rarely had fairies in them. Rather these stories are about things that happen to common people and often combined with a supernatural or magical element.

Myths and Legends

Myths and Legends, on the other hand, were usually stories about the Gods or the powerful, Kings and Queens were the central figures. These are epic tales and sagas full of cultural heroes and sometimes tragic in nature.

Animal stories

Where the central figures are animals but who can often talk and think and have to face very human dilemmas.

Fables and Parables

Both short stories which often conclude with a moral or lesson. A fable may differ from a parable in that it may contain anthropomorphised or magical elements such as talking objects or animals.

Family stories

Stories that are handed down across generations in families. These might be stories that go back over a hundred years to more recent stories involving sometimes major events like wars or more personal recollections. Such stories from the history of one's family are important not only in the social history but in forming a sense of identity. The telling makes sure they are not forgotten.

Anecdotes

A short, usually humorous account of an event. Often anecdotes might involve actual people either famous or known to us.

Homilies

A short story, like a sermon, with some moral or inspirational element, often spiritual in nature.

language and communication and it is a vital role of the parent of a young child to tell such stories. It is often the children who need it most who receive it least. Many people who work with stories often comment that children with emotional and behavioural difficulties respond with greatest enthusiasm to storytelling. It certainly appears they respond best to this type of communication, and they may do because they need it. Stories can also involve wordplay through puns, riddles, alliterations, proverbs, rhymes and rhythms. Such playing with words can invoke a love of language.

- **Cognitive** – cognition refers to thought and thinking skills. Language plays a significant part of this but it also includes such skills as attention and concentration, problem-solving skills, memory, beliefs and attitudes as well as predictive and analytical skills both verbal and non-verbal. On a most basic level, listening skills are needed which are developed through attention. Hearing the use of words in context helps develop vocabulary which in turn extends cognitive ability. The narrative thread of a story aids remembering through the use of both visualisation and linking of events that happens in listening to a story. Stories help develop reasoning skills such as identifying the self-contained 'logic' or truthfulness in a story. This does not mean whether a story is true or not.

Stories, for both adults and children, are enjoyed not because they are 'true or false', that is fact or fantasy, but if they have integrity and authenticity. Stories can help develop thinking skills as children quickly pick up the 'rules' or internal logic of a story. For instance, as children grow older they will need to have more sophisticated reasons if the laws of physics are broken – if someone travels in time there needs to be a time machine to do this or some kind of reason by which this becomes possible even in a make-believe world. If inanimate objects or animals can talk, there needs to be at least an implicit acknowledgement that the story exists in a 'different' place. Stories also develop visualisation skills. Stories paint pictures in people's minds as they listen. Visual imaging exists as an important part of our imagination (indeed, the word 'imagination' shares the same root as 'image'). Images can also help develop memory skills. Riddles and proverbs can also help the development of problem-solving, reasoning skills and help develop wisdom. Such learning can be enhanced by discussion of the conflicts, dilemmas and strategies used to solve problems in the story.

Stories have always had a role in helping understanding life, of giving answers to such questions as where do we come from and who are we. They can also help us understand behaviour and help link actions and consequences in a safe way. In this way they assist 'cause and effect' thinking. The process of listening is not passive but active, the meaning is made in the listener's mind.

- **Social and Emotional** - Both social and emotional aspects of development are connected and considered together. This is because these two aspects of development are particularly intertwined with each other. Emotional development takes place in the context of the relationships in our lives, and these relationships impact on emotions and how a person sees himself. Stories help us understand emotions, and give us a language for being able to recognise and think about them. This allows us to develop an 'inner mind' that helps us make sense of the world. Stories also help give us insight into the minds of others. Many stories can talk about psychological experiences, what people are feeling and how that influences them, stories can talk about inner motivations and desires, how people solve problems that can make things better, or perhaps worse. Stories give valuable information about how to relate to each other, they help explain and reinforce social rules and the effects of our actions on others. For example, the story of 'The Fearsome Giant', (see page 66) tells very clearly through story form how anxiety can be overcome by facing the source of the anxiety rather than avoiding it. The story explains this in a more powerful way than direct instruction or explanation ever can.

Stories will interact with internal psychological processes. The listener may identify with the protagonist of a story (which is why in many traditional stories details about characters are vague, increasing the potential for identification). Stories can circumvent our defence mechanisms and overcome resistance to change and therefore influence and change our beliefs.

There is increasing recognition of the importance of facilitating social and emotional development and skills in school settings. This is reflected in the UK Government's initiatives on ensuring school's in England address the 'Social and Emotional Aspects of Learning' (SEAL). It is the development of skills in these two domains that is central to Emotional Literacy, so these areas are explored in greater detail in Chapters 2 and 3 particularly.

- **Moral** – Children develop in their capacity to think about moral issues. The youngest children tend to think of morality in terms of the consequences, if you do something wrong you should get punished and be rewarded for doing something right. As the child grows into middle childhood, their understanding of morality is based on social conformity and the approval and disapproval of others, especially those in authority. In adolescence it becomes possible to develop a more abstract understanding of moral principles. Individual conscience becomes fully developed (7). So the emotional responses of young people will reflect their stage of moral development. Again, a story can act as a stimulus to help children develop thinking skills in regard to ethical and moral issues as stories can explore complexities, different perspectives and help children understand consequences of actions upon others. Children always have an innate interest in 'fairness' and this develops into a need for justice and a belief in a 'just world'. Stories can both gratify this belief and strengthen hope that things will turn out well in the end, and can also give the opportunity to question and examine this belief.

- **Spiritual** – It should be no surprise that teaching stories exist in all of the major religions, they are powerful tools in developing self and universal knowledge and wisdom. Such stories, that often contain creation stories or stories about the lives of significant figures, are used not only to educate about the major traditions but also are about enactments of key values of the religion. Often the key values transcend any particular religious 'group' and suggest key human characteristics essential to live peaceably. Such values as compassion, forgiveness, and tolerance of others are often advocated. It is interesting to note that these values are now being seen as significant in enhancing people's levels of psychological well-being. However, in our current cultural climate, these values are often forgotten and fear and mistrust of different religions and races as well as prejudice are becoming dominant. Such spiritual stories are still important, not so much as to promote any one particular religious belief but to promote wisdom and compassion and also understanding of different cultures and traditions. Indeed, in the multi-cultural society in which there is now an extraordinarily rich repertoire of stories from different traditions with striking similarities and differences the telling of these stories can do much to enhance the benefits of living together.

All these aspects of development are, of course, interconnected. They weave with each other, and with our physical and biological capabilities, create together what can be described as **self or whole-person development**. That these aspects of our personality interrelate leads to an integrated self or personality – a key feature of a mature and socially able and responsible adult capable of being a responsible member of the community. This aspect of development must remain one of the highest goals of education. Some commentators have argued that stories, particularly traditional or fairy stories, are metaphors for our internal world which act out aspects of our personality. Characters such as the evil witch, giant or ogre contrast with the beautiful Princess or handsome Prince, the wise woman or wizard and even the poor, smallest and unfavoured child who must overcome the greatest obstacles to succeed. Yet these characters reflect our inner world and our own constructions of self. Somehow we instinctively know that these stories are not about a literal truth. When the protagonist of a tale succeeds in his quest and marries the beautiful princess, receives untold wealth and lives 'happily ever after' we know what this really signifies is happiness in the here and now (8). That the protagonist succeeds through the application of such positive traits such as compassion, guile or quick-wittedness, bravery or perseverance teaches us unconsciously that these strengths can serve us well and put our own world to rights.

The Storyteller in the Classroom

Many of the powerful aspects of narrative and story can of course be gained from reading, or hearing stories being read aloud or experiencing stories through dramas on TV or at the cinema. However, when a story is told, as opposed to being read, it offers something very different. A storyteller engages the listener in a much more active way of relating. Storytelling exists in a social context. The story is told person to person. Eye contact can be made, gesture and intonation can intensify the experience of listening, the audience is much more connected with the story and the storyteller. The storyteller can readily, often intuitively, adapt the material of the story to suit the audience and the audience can communicate their reaction back to the teller. An old proverb, from the Scottish traveller people says, *"A story is told eye to eye, mind to mind and heart to heart."* When a teacher uses stories in the classroom they help children engage in the learning process, the teacher can match the content to the children's readiness to learn. Stories provide a way for a teacher to talk about emotional dilemma and conflicts in ways that children can identify with. They learn that they are not alone and that even the most difficult problems have solutions. Whilst they do this, many skills that will help their development are being practised.

Stories, of course, can be enhanced through reading, writing, discussion, role-play and drama, puppetry and so on. The potential of storytelling is dynamic and infinite in its possibilities. Storytelling is a powerful tool of learning that can be applied in a wide range of subjects. To tell a story well to a group of people may seem to some to be a daunting task and many people may not think themselves sufficiently skilled. At its best, storytelling is an art form and to bring professional storytellers into the school can be an invaluable experience. However, it is important not to see it as an elite skill that can be practised only by a talented few. Teachers use storytelling techniques all the time. Storytelling is a skill that belongs to us all - it needs practice and effort certainly - but for teachers it is an essential skill in guiding not only a child's learning but also his/her development into a mature young person. Experience in storytelling and practice will lead to an individual's development in this important skill. Everybody has the potential to be a storyteller as well as a listener and with sufficient practice this skill can be 'as natural as breathing'.

Notes

The quote from Philip Pullman comes, with permission, from the website of the Cambridge School Classics Project, a research and development project of the University of Cambridge. www.cambridgescp.com/page.php?p=mas%5Ewar_w_t%5Ereviews

(1)   The functions of storytelling presented here was inspired, and very much influenced by, a presentation by Robin Gwyndaf, Curator of Folklore at St Fagans Natural History Museum, Cardiff, which he gave to the Society for Storytelling Annual Gathering in 1997.

(2)   Margot Sunderland wrote this in her book, **'Using Storytelling as a Therapeutic Tool with Children'** (Speechmark, 2001).

(3)   This quote from Jack Zipes came from his foreword to **'Storytelling and Theatre'** by Mike Wilson (Palgrave, 2005).

(4)   From **'Storytelling in Education'** (The Society for Storytelling).

(5)   Alida Gersie (1991). **'Earthtales: Storytelling in times of change'** Green Print.

(6)   See Carol Fox's book, **'At the Very Edge of the Forest - the influence of literature on storytelling by children'** (Cassell Education, 1993).

(7)   This brief summary of moral development is based on the work of Lawrence Kohlberg.

(8)   Jon Kabat-Zinn (2004), **'Wherever You Go, There You Are'** (Piatkus Books, 2004).

2 - The Foundations of Emotional Literacy

"A lesson to draw from the entire literature on successful early interventions is that it is the social skills and motivation of the child that are easily altered – not IQ. These social and emotional skills affect performance in school and in the workplace. We too often have a bias towards believing that only cognitive skills are of fundamental importance to success in life. Our best long term investment is human capital investment in the form of emotional, social and cognitive education. To date, we are failing the first two areas of development in our educational systems."

Dr James Heckman, Nobel Laureate for Economic Sciences, 2000.

"Fish swim, birds fly and people feel."

Hiam Ginot

To what extent should schools be a place not just for promoting understanding but a place to be understood? This question is important as a child's emotional and social functioning plays a significant part in influencing how they will learn and behave in school and at home. After all, it is our capacity to experience a rich and complex emotional life that makes us most human. We are capable of feeling great love and joy in our lives, grief at the loss of someone we love deeply, rage and passion, shame and guilt if we behave badly.

Emotional Literacy in education concerns the domain of how children feel about themselves, their lives and relationships, both with peers and adults. Emotional functioning is a key factor in a child's well-being, how the child feels about him or herself in relation to learning and to others. It is not just important to children with emotional or learning problems but to all children. Emotional Literacy is about helping all children feel happier, better about themselves and better able to get on with others. From this, the person is better able to learn. Helping children learn to get on with others is increasingly recognized as a key skill they will need in adult life. Also, being better able to deal with feelings and relate to others, will lead to less behaviour problems and more co-operation in the classroom. There is also increasing recognition that emotional difficulties in children are hampering their learning. Emotional problems can adversely affect a child's academic and social development in a number of ways. They can lead to mental health problems and these are recognised as becoming more common in schools. Emotional problems and concerns can underlie problem behaviour and there are more and more children becoming disaffected with school life and seeing it as part of the problem and not part of the solution. Children in Secondary schools particularly are becoming unhappier at school and their education might be suffering. Helping young people remain engaged with education is critical.

With this recognition that our emotional lives are important to learning, Governments in the UK and elsewhere are putting an emphasis on schools and agencies that work with children to attend to their general well-being. The Green Paper 'Every Child Matters' has outlined a new approach to the well-being of children and young people from birth to age 19 which require all organisations who work with children to find new ways of co-operating together with other agencies and with children themselves with the key purpose of ensuring that children;

- Are healthy – both physically and emotionally.
- Stay safe – from both physical and emotional harm.
- Are able to experience enjoyment and achievement.
- Make a positive contribution to their communities.
- Are able to achieve economic well-being.

Schools that value emotional literacy in their practice are able to be more aware of the ways that they can help children feel safer and better about themselves in the learning situation. They can also help develop children's thinking and social skills to increase a sense of well-being and cooperation in the learning environment. Storytelling is a powerful way of helping children develop emotional and social competency and for the school as a whole to become a more emotionally sensitive and aware environment.

What is Emotional Literacy?

Emotional Literacy (EL) is about a person's ability to think about their own emotions and those of others and it has been defined in a number of ways.

- People are able to recognize, understand and appropriately express their emotions. (1)

- The practice of thinking individually and collectively about how emotions shape our actions and of using emotional understanding to enrich our thinking. (2).

- The capacity in individuals and groups to perceive and understand and manage emotions in oneself and in others. (3)

It is very much connected to the concept of 'emotional intelligence', which was described by Daniel Goleman in his book, 'Emotional Intelligence - Why Can It Matter More Than IQ' (4). Emotional intelligence is about the capacity to think about and manage feelings, in ourselves and others, and to be able to motivate ourselves positively. It has been applied to organisations at work, physical and mental health, and schools. The terms emotional intelligence and emotional literacy are often used interchangeably, however, EL is used to describe the application of emotional intelligence in education, particularly in the UK. There are three main outcomes of emotional literacy strategies and these are intended to benefit all children not just those with emotional and behavioural difficulties.

- **Academic learning** – helping create the right emotional climate in schools. Helping children manage feelings has had demonstrable benefits in helping children learn academic skills. Emotional understanding can deepen academic understanding.

- **Improving behaviour and co-operation** – as children become better able to express and manage feelings and conflicts with others there will be improvements in behaviour and motivation to work and co-operation increases.

16

- **Well-being is enhanced** – feelings of personal confidence and self-esteem improve when children's feelings are respected and when their competencies are acknowledged. Developing EL builds resilience and aids mental health.

Placing social and emotional learning on the curriculum is relatively new in the UK but is more advanced in the US and there is considerable evidence of the effectiveness of such programmes. Interventions across the age span consider such skills as self-awareness, emotional management, perspective-taking and build in complexity and sophistication as children grow older. An Evaluation by the Collaborative for Academic, Social and Emotional Learning (CASEL) has found evidence that such interventions not only lead to differences in behaviour such as decreased verbal and physical aggression, less truanting, an increase in co-operative and helping behaviours. There was also significant increases in academic achievement. The reasons for these gains in learning skills remains unclear, but it may be that increased awareness of others feelings leads to a safer school environment and better problem solving skills. Also, closer bonds with teachers and peers may enhance motivation. Such skills in listening, self-motivation and management are also wanted by employers. Ultimately, social and emotional learning may help to develop socially responsible adults. Programmes, such as the FRIENDS Programme are being introduced into the UK and again there is evidence as to the benefits of such education in creating calmer classrooms, confident children and safer schools.

At the heart of emotional literacy there is a focus on relationships. Relationships are valued and individuals are respected, and this is most evident in the communication that takes place between members of the school. Speaking and listening skills are clearly important here and what characterises emotional literacy most is when there is a meaningful dialogue going on between people. It should now be clear that emotional literacy is fostered in an environment where people are able to reflect on our thoughts and feelings and actions. The climate of the school is one where all members are valued. Developing emotional literacy is helped by an understanding of the five key pathways in which all, both adults and children, are continually developing.

The Five Key Pathways of Emotional Literacy

Much as one might see good exercise, diet and lifestyle as laying the foundations for good physical health there are a number of key dimensions or pathways that aid mental health, well being and build resilience. These pathways contribute to our overall abilities in emotional literacy. The five key pathways are self-awareness, managing emotions, motivation, empathy and social competence and are described below (5). 'These pathways are the key areas identified in the UK Government's *Social and Emotional Aspects of Learning (SEAL)* programme.'

Self-awareness

Self-awareness refers to a person's ability to know their own emotional state - to be able to recognise what feelings are being experienced at any one time and to be aware of the thoughts that are involved in this. Like all the pathways, the capacity to do this develops over time and the objective of this is to have a **positive, integrated sense of self** where we see ourselves as competent and caring. One of the key skills necessary for this is to have an **emotional vocabulary** which reflects our emotional experience. Without words for our feelings we are less able to reflect on them and more likely to act them out in our behaviour. The young person able to name how others make them feel and why is going to be more able to solve problems with peers than one who can only say 'I hate you' when annoyed by others.

The awareness of one's own feelings is a key component of well-being. If we are aware of how we think and feel, it increases the choices that are open to us. Children develop in this capacity as they grow older, and having an emotional vocabulary is an important part of this. Often children will develop a sophisticated emotional vocabulary in their interactions at home and at school. However, many young people may not develop this perhaps due to the quality of the interactions at home, to specific educational difficulties or a combination of the two. Mindfulness of the importance of acknowledging, respecting and talking about feelings aids communication. When feelings are acknowledged people feel understood. Stories of all kinds are particularly useful as a way of recognising and validating feelings.

Managing Emotions (Self-Regulation)

We all experience emotions and strong feelings will give us an impulse to act in a certain way. We need to be able to manage our feelings effectively particularly such emotions as anxiety, anger and sadness to ensure we are not overwhelmed or just act them out. If emotions go out of control, we can lose control of our actions, they can dominate our mood or lead to emotional and mental health difficulties such as depression. We also need to recognise and facilitate positive emotions in ourselves so that we can relax and make ourselves happy. There are a number of key skills we need to be able to develop in managing emotions, some children will learn all these skills easily, others will struggle with some of them. Key skills include **the ability to calm oneself** when experiencing strong feelings – this may include seeking a source of safety or delaying one's response rather than acting on impulse. Other key skills are **tolerating frustration** and **being able to think creatively and flexibly for new solutions.** This will include seeking sources of help. Children can be helped in learning these skills appropriately at school. This does not mean intruding inappropriately into their private lives, but addressing things that happen in the classroom, with peers and with or in dealing with behaviour as emotional issues often underlie behaviour problems. School is a fantastic place to learn these key skills in managing emotions. Again, stories give great opportunities to help learn these skills as they often describe how characters feel, how it makes them act and to see the consequences of their actions.

Motivation

Motivation is key for learning and it is essential to be able to motivate oneself to achieve one's goals. Approval from adults is often a key motivator for younger children and as they grow older they will develop more internal motivation as they begin to see further into the future and can work towards their goals, dreams and hopes. It is having

THE PRIMARY COLOURS OF EMOTION

It is, perhaps, our complex emotional life that makes us most human. There are over 1500 words for emotions and feelings in the English language. However, these different words can be grouped into a much smaller set of different emotion groups. It is now accepted that our emotions influence our thinking, decisions and behaviour. And they can do so, both positively and negatively. Our emotions can also run out of our control, and we can be taken over by feelings of panic, anger or even excitement. Emotional literacy is not about denying our feelings, it is about accepting, even welcoming them, and in so doing, understanding them. This way we can use our emotions positively rather than being consumed by or acting them out.

Our emotional life is the product of evolution, and all of the emotions we feel have a function. Emotions are physical, psychological and social in nature. There is a biological component as when we experience strong feelings there are physical changes in the body. Emotions are also psychological in that they both influence and are influenced by thinking and behaviour. Finally, there is a social component as emotions are influenced by other people and are part of the bonds that we form in our relationships.

All of our emotions lead us to behave in certain ways, and even difficult emotions play a role in our survival. Children are going to experience emotions in learning situations that will serve to motivate them to either learn more or to avoid certain situations. Our complex emotional life results from a smaller group of emotions, which blend together like primary colours, to produce the full spectrum of our emotional repertoire. This group consists of anxiety/fear, anger/irritation, happiness/joy, sadness/grief and disgust/hatred. There is also the influence of love and attachment on emotional development as well.

Anxiety - encompasses a group of emotions from worry and caution through to terror and fear. Anxiety is important for us, because it alerts us to danger in the immediate environment and helps us to assess the risk in a situation. However, too much anxiety can be overwhelming. Learning is difficult to take place if there is too much anxiety and children always need to feel safe and secure for them to explore the world. Strategies such as facing and overcoming fear, avoiding or running away from danger and seeking out sources of help are all illustrated in stories.

Anger - is another way of responding to danger and threat, and as such may be a way of dealing with underlying anxiety. Anger is often seen as a negative or unacceptable emotion. However, it is not the emotion itself that is the problem. It is how we manage it. Anger helps us to stand up for and assert ourselves. It can be a reaction to a perceived injustice and trigger action. Of course the problem with anger is that it can lead to aggression and destruction. Common methods of dealing with anger are aggression and passivity where angry thoughts are bottled up and maybe taken out on something else. Yet being assertive is the most effective way of standing up for oneself without attacking others. A key skill is learning to wait and delay one's response to anger even for a few seconds until the full strength of the emotion has passed and it can be acted upon more thoughtfully. Anger can lead to renegotiation in a relationship.

Sadness - is a response to a loss and change, and an inevitable part of life. The process of grief is an example of how it takes time to adapt to the loss, in this case the loss of a loved one. Crying can be a helpful way of expressing this feeling and also alert others that we may need help, sadness commonly elicits empathy in others. Sadness can lead to disengagement, reflection and reconsideration of oneself. However, sadness can be overwhelming to the point we can find no joy in ourselves and in extreme cases can lead to depression. (For some children, the term "sad" has now become one of derision.)

Happiness - is equally an important emotion to learn about, to know how to find and foster. Happiness and well-being is an important component of mental health and resilience. When children feel safe and secure, they are happy and more curious and able to engage in creative and collaborative playing. This, in turn, increases their feelings of competency and mastery in the world. There is now growing interest in the area of positive psychology, which is concerned with increasing happiness through developing our personal strengths and positive qualities (6).

Love and Attachment - The emotion of love is essential to our humanity and is intertwined with the bonds that we form with others. Our feelings of love can be traced back to our earliest attachments. It is in this early attachment relationship with the caregiver where the foundations of emotional literacy are developed. The degree of security and the caregiver's capacity to nurture us help develop an emotional language and understanding and sets a path for future development.

However, we carry on learning about how to manage feelings throughout life. And there are always times when we can be consumed by strong feelings that overwhelm us. Developing emotional literacy is about being able to think about feelings so that we are not so overwhelmed by them and to be better able to relate and communicate with others.

hope for the future that helps people both work academically and remain motivated to behave in the present. This means an ability to delay gratification. A young person scared of failure and with little faith in himself will have less motivation to work towards a desired imagined future. Rather their motivation may be to avoid difficulties and hardships in the present. Finding effective ways of building positive motivation is essential and this is an area where there has been much research which is beyond the scope of this book. Effective techniques for building motivation include the use of descriptive rather than evaluative praise and helping young people paint pictures in their mind's eye of what lays ahead of them. Also, understanding that more is achieved when co-operating with others is important as well as knowing the limits of competition as a motivator. It is not so important to be better than others but it is important to be able to beat one's own previous best. 'Intrinsic' motivation, that is a motivation driven from one's self, is more fulfilling than 'extrinsic' motivation, which comes from the external pressures and rewards to behave in certain ways. Stories, of course, can play a key part in building motivation.

Empathy

Empathy, or Social Perceptiveness, is the ability to see how others are thinking and feeling. To empathise is to see and understand another person's frame of reference or perspective. To be able to take another's perspective is a fundamental inter-personal skill that is essential in being able to get on well with and relate to others. The foundations of empathy are learnt in the infant's first emotional attachment to their primary caregiver. The caregiver gives the infant empathy and the child internalises this and the capacity to understand others develops. With this comes an ability to communicate and understand. Without it, a child may remain less aware or unaffected by the experiences of others. Specific learning difficulties such as Asperger's Syndrome and Autism can also lead to difficulties in the development of empathy. Such difficulties might also result from difficulties in attachment relationships. A sense of insecurity may impede the ability to see how others are actually thinking.

As a child grows, he/she can increasingly recognise that others think differently from how he/she does and can develop the capacity for understanding what and why other people are thinking and feeling. The child (or adult) who is aware of how their actions affect others gains confidence in him/herself as well as being better able to get on with others.

Being able to empathise with others is the foundation for being able to feel compassion and caring towards others. For a long time it was thought that empathy was an innate quality. However, it is now more accepted that it is possible for empathy to be developed in children, and in education settings. It can be encouraged by allowing children to be able to discuss their feelings and to have them listened to and accepted. Again, this is important for all children, it is critical for those who are having difficulties in understanding others. Repeated practice in being able to imagine and perceive another's perspective, through the use of stories, role-plays, debates and discussions, can help children develop their ability to see and understand different points of view.

Social Competence

Beyond empathy, there are interpersonal and social skills we need to get along with others and this involves being able to manage strong feelings in others and manage relationships. Children need to know when they have upset or made others angry and how they can help to rectify the situation; to be able to repair relationships. They also need to know when things are going well and experience joy in relationships. Children learn social skills in their everyday interactions, particularly in playing together. Using co-operative and structured games, particularly in activities like drama, are excellent for helping learn these skills. Such games naturally aid the development of social skills as they provide opportunities for such things as eye contact, turn-taking, understanding rules and negotiating conflict. Some children will have particular difficulties and need additional help, and well skilled children may benefit from learning high levels of assertion and conflict resolution skills. These skills in relationships are critical for our self-esteem and well-being. Developing friendship skills, social problem-solving skills, mediation and conflict resolution skills are important in helping children learn how to get along with others, meet their own needs in the context of mutually satisfying relationships. Stories are of course an excellent stimulus for discussion of strategies for getting along with others.

Communication Skills

It is through developing these skills in these five areas that emotional intelligence is facilitated. These skills develop throughout all of life, but it is during childhood and adolescence that learning is most accelerated. Schools are critical in helping this emotional growth and development. The particular contribution that storytelling can make in this is explored in Chapter 3. There are many ways that emotional literacy can be nurtured in the school environment. To be most effective, it needs to be part of the school ethos itself, where good relationships are valued and there is a focus on good communication. All our interactions with children, provided that they are respectful and valuing, offer the opportunity for children to develop and strengthen these skills. Particular communication skills help children develop their own ability to communicate and foster emotional literacy, these include reflective listening, positive feedback, problem-solving conversations, thinking skills, interpersonal skills and reflective practice. These are described below.

Reflective Listening

Reflective listening involves being able to listen with one's full attention to what another is saying, to be able to hear the emotional content and to reflect that back in a way that is helpful. Such listening lays the foundation for helping a person, particularly a child, experience being understood, and in having their feelings respected, feels validated. It also helps build the development of an emotional vocabulary. The skills involved are both simple and complex including questions, reflecting back what the person is saying and naming feelings. A reflective listener will often make many statements of understanding rather than explaining or reasoning continually with children. Teacher and psychologist, Hiam Ginott, who has often been described as the grandfather of emotional intelligence and a pioneer in adult-child communication has written extensively about how adults can help children manage and express feelings (7).

Positive Feedback

Giving positive and regular feedback encourages co-operation and motivation. It also boosts feelings of confidence and competence. This includes positive descriptive praise about what people are getting right and the effects it is having on others. Expectations are stated clearly, and when there are difficulties there are always opportunities given to the person to put things right. Comments that belittle or humiliate are not used. There is a focus on the consequences of both appropriate and inappropriate behaviour rather than an over reliance on sanctions and punishments for when people misbehave. When issues of behaviour need to be addressed they are dealt with quickly and assertively.

Problem-solving Conversations

Everybody faces problems all the time no matter who they are. Problem-solving conversations focus on helping children learn how to solve the problems in their lives and sort them out for themselves. To be able to deal with things that are frustrating or that cause disagreements and conflicts between friends can give children great confidence in themselves so that they can cope. In such a conversation there are several steps:

- A problem is defined
- Possible solutions might be brainstormed or considered
- Ideas are evaluated and a strategy is decided on
- The strategy is tried out and evaluated

These problem-solving conversations can be held with individual children or with groups and can be formal or informal. The adult would refrain from trying to solve problems too easily or rushing to answer questions, but will give the child space to try and think things through. For instance, one teacher used this technique to help two children who were arguing over sharing an item to consider how they could both get what they want. Another used it with a class to think about how they could all get on better with each other. Stories can give clear examples of how a problem can be thought through and the consequences of actions considered.

Thinking Skills

Developing thinking skills is being increasingly recognized as a critical learning skill. As well as acquiring knowledge it is important to be able to evaluate that knowledge. Skills in thinking can also be applied to our emotional lives to see if what we're thinking about our feelings makes sense. Exercises that develop skills in thinking flexibly, laterally or hypothetically, to be able to evaluate and collect evidence and take on different perspectives are all useful in developing emotional literacy. Using questions that guide and encourage are a key part in developing these skills and these questions can be a stimulus for enquiry. The teacher guides through questions that enquire and explore issues in a way that helps others do the same.

This helps children to:
- Ask questions and raise topics for discussion
- Develop their own ideas, views and theories
- Give reasons for what they think

- Explain and argue their point of view with others
- Listen to and consider the views of others
- Change their ideas in the light of good reasons and evidence (flexible thinking)

In social relationships children, like adults, can make thinking errors such as misunderstanding another's intentions. Being able to identify these can help sort out problems in relationships and in managing feelings. Unhelpful thinking styles can include focusing on another's negative qualities and discounting positives or thinking you know what someone else is thinking without checking it out. One can also make thinking errors about oneself, for instance, always predicting failure or being certain you know something for sure without confirmation. In storytelling, such questions can be used to stimulate thinking about the story and the thoughts and cognitions of characters can be explored to help identify helpful and unhelpful ways of thinking.

Developing Interpersonal Skills

Interpersonal skills can be developed in children to help them collaborate with each other and with adults in working together. One of the most important ways of developing such social skills is through games and structured play. These present plenty of opportunities for children to develop social confidence, to learn how to compromise and negotiate around disagreements, develop turn taking skills and to be able to give praise and encouragement to others. Such games can strengthen skills such as eye contact, appropriate touch and to be able to encourage others. Conflict resolution and mediation skills can be developed through peer counselling and peer support schemes and friendship skills can be discussed and talked about. Circle time, team building and group work exercises can also help develop the skills. Many of these exercises focus on how more can be achieved in working together than in working alone. Critical interpersonal skills include friendships skills, being friendly to other people, not tolerating bullying or making fun of others, being able to talk and listen to others, to be fun and kind, perhaps most importantly to be thoughtful of others.

Reflective Practice

What underlies many of the interpersonal skills just mentioned is that we are able to think about ourselves and to be aware of our own thoughts and actions as well of those of the young people. We need to be able to see the effect that we have upon others and be able to learn from our actions, mistakes as well as successes. Developing our own reflective practice, is one of the most important aspects of being able to help children develop their own emotional literacy. The more we understand about our own processes of thoughts and feelings, the more we can be helpful to others. Reflective practice can be done by oneself or with others, and it is perhaps through working with others in an atmosphere where one feels safe enough to be able to think together. This is also an important way of managing some of the stresses of working with children. It helps the quality of our relationships. By reflection, we can learn how to transform negative emotions into something more positive. Conversations with children and helping develop their own storytelling skills can foster their capacity for reflective thinking.

EMOTIONAL LITERACY REFLECTIVE ASSESSMENT

These questions are aimed at facilitating thinking about where a child may be on the pathways of EL. There are no right or wrong answers and answers will depend on a child's age and stage of development, but can identify strengths and areas to work on.

Self-awareness
- Does the child have a full emotional vocabulary to cover a range of emotions - particularly well-being, fear, anger and sadness?
Does the child have a positive and consistent view of him or herself? Does this extend over a variety of situations, home, classroom, playground, peers?
Can the child verbalise (or express through other means such as play or creative activity) both positive and negative feelings reflecting his/her emotional state?

Emotion Regulation
- Is the child able to be soothed and calmed in the face of distressing feelings through helpful interactions with others?
Is the child able to soothe and calm themselves in the face of strong feelings, including frustration, through their own efforts. What 'scripts' do they have for different emotions?
Does the child demonstrate self-control or do they generally tend to be impulsive?

Motivation
- Does the child respond better to external motivators (praise/rewards) or to more internal motivations (sense of achievement/mastery/well-being)?
Is the child reacting more towards positive reinforcers (where there may be gains, both material or psychological in nature) or negative reinforcers (i.e. to avoid anxieties, losses or perceived failures)?

Is the child able to work towards future orientated or longer term goals and able to delay gratification to achieve them?

Empathy
- Is the child able to feel compassion towards someone who is distressed. Is s/he able to offer comfort?
Does the child demonstrate an understanding of how others are thinking or feeling?
Is the child soothed or calmed when s/he feels understood by others?

Social Problem-solving skills
- Is the child able to understand and be sensitive to social rules in a variety of situations (playing with friends/working collaboratively on tasks/taking turns and sharing)?
Is the child able to make and maintain relationships with peers on a one to one and group levels (friendship skills)?
Is the child able to negotiate and manage conflict and resolve disagreements, do they escalate or de-escalate situations (conflict resolution skills)?

Emotional Literacy and Narrative Theory

"Maybe there are only three kinds of stories: the stories we live, the stories we tell, and the higher stories that help our souls fly up towards the greater light."

Ben Okri, 'Birds of Heaven'
Weidenfield & Nicholson, 1995

Emotional literacy cannot be thought about just as something that might be developed in children without considering the context of the environment. Emotional literacy is all about dialogue, about people talking and listening to each other with respect for each others' experience. In this sense, it involves listening to the stories that we tell and retell each other about ourselves and our lives. Narrative theory is very much concerned with the notion of how we store knowledge and beliefs in the stories we have and tell to each other. What is most important is the story we have about ourselves and the extent we feel able to write or rewrite that story or whether it is written solely by others. The conversations we have with each other and with children in school shapes our perceptions of reality and how people see themselves. So it is then that we want the stories and narratives of people to be narratives of hope, optimism and influence, where they can see themselves as competent, problem-solvers and able to care for others. It helps if we have a good story to tell and that we have the confidence to tell it. Storytelling can help us to do that, and in so doing helps develop our emotional literacy skills essential to living.

Notes

The quote from James Heckman comes, with permission, from the website
www.builinitiative.org/pdf/Heckman2.pdf
(Also published by the Ounce of Protection Fund and University of Chicago School of Public Policy Studies)

The quote from Hiam Ginot comes, with permission, from 'Between Parent and Child' (Three Rivers Press, 2003)

(1) **'Nurturing Emotional Literacy'** by Peter Sharp (David Fulton Publishers, 2001).

(2) **'The Emotional Literacy Handbook'** produced by Antidote – the campaign for Emotional Literacy (David Fulton Publishers, 2003)

(3) **'Emotional Literacy at the Heart of the School Ethos'** by Steve Killick (Sage/Lucky Duck, 2006)

(4) **'Emotional Intelligence – why it can matter more than IQ'** by Daniel Goleman (Bloomsbury, 1995)

(5) These are summarised from **Emotional Literacy at the Heart of the School Ethos** by Steve Killick (see note 3).

(6) **'Authentic Happiness'** by Martin Seligman (Nicolas Brearly Publishing, 2002)

(7) Hiam Ginott's books on adult child communication remain classics and although written over thirty years ago are still relevant today. **'Between Parent and Child'** (Three Rivers Press, 2003) and **'Teacher and Child'** (Avon Books, 1972) are particularly recommended.

3 - Connecting Storytelling and Emotional Literacy

"Grandmother told me many stories . . . At the time I thought that was all that they were, tales of animals and heroes. But she was teaching me humility, self-sacrifice, kindness, tolerance; looking back I can see how much she influenced me."

Sun Shuyun, 'Ten Thousand Miles without a Cloud.'
Harper Perennial, 2004

Storytelling then is not only a methodology in education but one that has particular application in developing emotional literacy. The use of stories to develop emotional and social competencies includes;

- The telling of tales either traditional or modern that emphasise values and qualities, perspective taking and offer an opportunity for reflection.

- Reading, writing and, of course, telling stories, either personal or fictional, that emphasise feelings or explore relationships.

- Using games, toys, puppets, drawings or other stimuli to help invent and tell stories.

- Using interactive stories to develop confidence, imagination and a sense of fun in the classroom.

- Targeting particular difficulties that young people might be having in social or educational skills.

Stories are such a useful way of talking about emotional and social aspects of living because they can talk about inner feelings and conflicts without intruding into the personal lives of children. In this way emotional matters are explored at a distance and through metaphor that allows children to find their own meanings in them. Stories offer the opportunity for both personal and shared reflection. Stories can be used as a stimulus for thinking and discussion and there will be many instances when they do not need to be interpreted or explained at all.

It should not be surprising that stories are so useful for emotional and social development. After all we actively seek out emotional experiences in many ways for instance reading books, watching movies or sporting events. Stories elicit emotional responses which is why we find them engaging. Actually telling a story amplifies that emotional response.

Stories can be used in many different situations, one-to-one, with whole classes to help engage in the subject and of course in larger or whole school events, such as assemblies. They break up and contrast well with the activities of instruction and moralistic teaching and they can be adapted to every age and level of ability.

Stories and the Five Pathways of Emotional Literacy

Stories can be useful in facilitating development of the five pathways of emotional literacy and develop particular emotional and social competencies.

Self-awareness

Stories build up the fundamental pathway of self-awareness through building an emotional vocabulary through to being able to discuss a 'sense of self'. Stories commonly use many emotion words, in context, which helps create meaning, and such use builds up an emotional vocabulary. An emotional vocabulary is essential for being able to process feelings in oneself and others and to learn that strong physical sensations and impulses belong to the phenomenon of emotion and can be an impulse to certain actions. It may seem that this learning comes readily and easily and is not something that needs to be done in formal education settings. Clearly much of the foundation for this is laid in the early years before a child begins school, but children vary greatly in their capacity to do this, and family backgrounds will also vary widely. The foundations of all the dimensions of emotional literacy are laid in the attachment relationship, but all experiences a young person has can help develop their understanding of self. Often therapeutic work with children with emotional problems starts with helping build the emotional vocabulary and understanding.

Stories build an emotional vocabulary that is essential for being aware of the feelings that one has, through naming feelings. In the story, 'The Fearsome Giant,' (see page 66) the young hero of the tale is described as having 'a very large knot in his stomach and his legs were like jelly'. This helps the child know about the physical sensations of emotion, in this case anxiety and the storyteller can reinforce this through the tone of her voice, gesture and facial expression. The non-verbal body language reinforces the meaning of the emotion.

It is in reflection and discussion of the story that the potential for emotional understanding is increased. Exploring and discussing stories can build on this understanding of the inner world necessary for self-awareness and this can be facilitated by such questions as:

What was the character feeling?

What made him feel like that?

How else might he have felt?

What was he thinking?

Such questions can help build an understanding about the relationship between thoughts and feelings, that our perceptions and beliefs can influence our feelings and we can find different ways of thinking. Stories can tell how characters can feel about themselves and give examples of both positive and negative statements about the self and the effects they can have on feelings. The teller can help set the scene for creating safe and reflective conversations by discussing their own feelings and reactions to the story acknowledging that there are different ways the story can be understood. The best discussion is often liveliest when the questions do not have a right or wrong answer and different perspectives are heard.

Self-regulation (or emotion management)

Being able to manage our own feelings is a vital part of well being; to be able to soothe and calm ourselves, or to find someone we can trust who can help us is important in dealing with anxiety and fears. To be able to control our impulses to hurt others either psychologically or physically is important in dealing with the impulse of anger. It is important to know how to manage anger and frustration assertively rather than through aggression and to be able to delay acting impulsively when one is engulfed in strong feelings.

One most useful skill is to know when to seek counsel. Learning how to deal with loss and change is another area where keys skills are developed in childhood. Many children have to deal with significant losses during the period of growing-up. When one has to deal with loss, it is important to be able to allow oneself to grieve, to experience the impact of the loss and to give oneself time to adapt and grow from the pain.

It is important to know the value of happiness and to know how to pursue it; to know how to cultivate pleasure and enjoy oneself rather than be overwhelmed by feelings or boredom or unspecified anxiety. Being able to play is one of the principal means by which children achieve this. Storytelling, story-making and listening are all components of active play. Play is an activity that builds important personal aspects and the ability to do this remains important not just in childhood, but also throughout life.

Stories can help children to learn strategies for dealing with emotions through hearing what happens with others. Listeners identify with the characters in the stories and can learn from the positive actions. When the story is told, rather than read, and possibly even chosen because of its aptness for the listeners, its potential for learning is increased. Again, the teller can emphasise through their telling or reflective dialogue the emotional transformations that take place in the story.

The process of listening to stories from a positive figure in one's life is in itself a soothing and relaxing activity. For parents and children storytelling times together are moments of intimacy and bonding – a key attachment activity. It is no coincidence that stories are told and read before one goes to sleep. On the threshold of a dream world, stories prepare and relax and build a psychologically safe internal world.

Some might worry that the content of stories should not be scary for children, and of course, stories should be pitched at a level that is appropriate. But stories do offer the opportunity to learn to achieve mastery of emotions like fear and children love scary stories for this reason. Many of the original traditional folk and fairy stories of many cultures are quite frightening affairs populated with monsters or witches. These stories were meant to scare as well as entertain and to help the listeners learn about dealing with danger. In the end the forces of 'evil' are defeated and the child gains knowledge of the dangers of the world in metaphorical form. Of course, the **intention** of the storyteller is critical – the storyteller does not wish to traumatise, but to give an experience that is both exciting and safe and leads to a resolution. The storyteller can also respond to the reactions of the audience, intensifying the emotion if the audience is actively engaged or lessening if this experience is becoming overwhelming.

Stories can build the connection between understanding the links between feelings, the behaviours they lead to and the consequences of those actions. This can be particularly so in thinking about the emotion of anger – and about learning about the consequences of acting aggressively or constructively in response to this feeling. Often stories present opportunities to think how anger can lead to reactions of impulsive aggression and violence or timidity, when a person does nothing except ruminate on angry and resentful feelings. The story of 'Gelert the Dog' (see page 104) reveals a man who, in a rage, kills his beloved dog after jumping to a conclusion rather than finding out the 'whole story'. Stories can give demonstrations of assertive or forgiving actions, how anger and resentment can be transformed through patience, reflection and understanding. Contemporary stories can be effective in doing this as well and stories about children and young people can provide good examples for thinking about complex social situations and learning how to act justly can be useful.

Sadness, loss and bereavement is another area of emotional management that can be facilitated through stories. Many stories which children will be familiar explore these themes, such as J.K. Rowling's Harry Potter series and E.B. White's 'Charlottes Web'. Sadness is both a natural and adaptive response to loss that helps us adjust and change, and stories are particularly effective in articulating and validating these feelings. Losses can be difficult to talk about and the 'distance' provided by stories allows for a safe emotional expression and containment. Healthy – leads us to adapt – sad stories can be quite moving bringing us into touch with sadness and help us learn the natural process. Of course, this is a theme that is commonly touched upon in literature. Eileen Jones (2001) has written about how such stories can be helpful for bereaved children and compiled a list of stories and books that deal with this subject (1).

The anxiety or fear of loss of parents is also a common theme that emerges in children's fiction and manifests itself in an interest in what would happen to children without parents and how they might find guardians to look after them. This theme emerges in many fairy tales and also more recent stories such as 'Peter Pan' or 'The Jungle Book'.

Motivation

Many traditional tales are about an ordinary person, usually a child, perhaps the youngest or most unfortunate in a family, who is faced with an obstacle or challenge. Somehow, they persevere and through determination, wit or good fortune brought about through kindness, manage to succeed. Their reward is often untold wealth and, sometimes, even marriage into royalty! Most often, the implication is that they will live happily ever after. This, of course, is not presented as a reality, no one lives happily ever after, but rather it is a metaphor that difficulties can be overcome and all can be well in the 'here and now' of the present. A satisfying story offers hope that things will improve and it is worth the effort of tolerating and persevering through difficulty to achieve longer-term goals. To reach such goals requires healthy and strong motivation. Stories gently imbed suggestions in the listener's minds of hopefulness in the future, the effort and delayed gratification is worthwhile.

Stories also offer the opportunity to explore the motivations of the characters and thus learn more about psychological actions and help to learn about one's own intentions and those of others. This capacity to develop insight is also relevant to all the pathways of emotional literacy.

USING STORIES TO DEVELOP EMOTIONAL CONTROL AND DECISION-MAKING

There are increasing numbers of stories written to help young people develop particular aspects of emotional development such as anger management or decision-making. Many of these can be used in one to one or classroom or group situations. Although these stories are designed to be read either by the student themselves or to be read aloud, they are very suitable for adapting and being 'told' as opposed to read.

One story was specifically designed to help children from between seven and twelve learn about controlling anger. 'The Bubblegum Guy' by Joost Dorst (2) tells of a child born with a piece of bubblegum in his mouth, but when he gets angry this bubblegum blows up into an enormous bubble, then bursts spraying bubblegum over everybody. No matter what he does, he cannot get rid of this bubble gum and its disastrous effects. The story tells of how he finally learns that he can do something. The story is interspersed with opportunities for reflection and there are worksheets designed to help children understand how anger can affect them and what they can do to control it. Research into interventions has found this to be effective in helping children learn emotional control skills.

The 'Life Choices' series uses stories to help children think about decision-making. Using stories based on situations with friends, peers and adults that children and young people might face and that present real dilemmas, the series aims to help build decision making skills. Effective decision-making needs a recognition of thoughts and feelings and an ability to consider consequences and alternatives and to evaluate these to choose the best outcome. The series includes stories for infant, junior and adolescent children. Phil Carradice's (2006) 'Life Choices' is aimed at Secondary school children and includes stories that young people will relate to that explore such themes as stealing, bullying, prejudice, attraction and love amongst others. These stories can be followed by creative activities such as creative writing or discussion to explore these themes (3).

An essential part of understanding one's motivation is to know that we can often be full of conflicting or mixed feelings that can present us with dilemmas. For instance, one may feel attracted towards another person yet fear rejection, or one might want to give up smoking because of worries about the risk to health yet also enjoy the sensations and experience of smoking. Such conflicts of feelings may affect one's actions. In exploring the conflicts and dilemmas that characters face in stories we can learn about motivation, when one is considering, avoiding or ready to embark on a course of action or to make a change in one's life.

Empathy

Empathy is about social perceptiveness and the ability to see another's point of view as different from one's own. It is also to see the validity of that point of view. Empathy is a prerequisite for compassion and kindness. It should be evident at this point how stories give insight into the psychological worlds of others and in so doing increases the listeners ability to understand what another is thinking and feeling and to know that another person can see the world differently. There is evidence that reading literature can increase and develop one's ability to empathise. Although oral storytelling has not been as thoroughly researched as reading, there is no reason to believe that it would be any less effective. Indeed, storytelling, being based in an active relationship between teller and listener may be more effective as the teller can respond to the reactions of the listeners.

Again, we all vary in our capacity to be able to empathise with others. Some do this easily and can convey this understanding readily, others may find it more difficult. Girls, on average, may be more empathic than boys and empathy aids effective communication, we can relate better and adjust our message to help it be understood. From an evolutionary perspective it is now thought that the ability to empathise preceded and laid the foundations for language to develop. Daniel Goleman called empathy 'the fundamental people skill' as it is critical in good communication. As so many jobs now involve working with people and the 'service industries' are on the increase, it is important to cultivate this ability to empathise with others. We also know that an individual's ability to be able to empathise may be affected by both genetic and social factors. It is also clear that empathic skills can be developed through education. Empathy can be developed through discussions about feelings, exploring ways of taking different perspectives, for example exploring other cultures or communities. Practise in taking another person's point of view assists empathy development as does hearing the stories of particularly compassionate and empathic people such as Mahatma Gandhi or Martin Luther King. Clearly through stories we see, in our mind's eye, how others see things and how things can be different.

Social Competence (managing emotions in others)

Developing social skills to deal with the complex world of relationships is an important part of growing up – and is something we are always learning about throughout life. For children and young people this is very important and to feel liked is a major contributor to feelings of confidence. How a child gets on with her friends may be a greater influence on her feelings of well-being than other areas of life such as academic work. Friendships and relationships with siblings with the continual

USING 'SOCIAL STORIES' TO DEVELOP SOCIAL UNDERSTANDING

Some children have particular difficulties in aspects of social communication – particularly in developing empathy. A technique known as 'Social Stories' has been found to be very effective in helping children develop an understanding of social rules. It was designed for children who are often described as having Asperger's Syndrome or Autistic Spectrum Disorder, but the technique may be helpful, with adaptation, to all children who are having particular difficulties with understanding others and/or are lacking some social skills.

Such children (who might appear rude or angry, actually might have difficulties in impulse control or understanding how others think or feel) can be helped to gain greater understanding of situations by having stories specially written for them that help them gain an understanding of the situation and suggest what might be appropriate behaviours. These stories, described by Carol Gray (2004), can also be helpful to let others understand the perspective of the child.

The technique involves creating a short story about an event that presents difficulty to the child and where he may have difficulty in understanding about what is the correct thing to do. An example may be the child who has problems queuing appropriately for lunch. A story is developed after talking with the child about how he sees the problem and discovering what is confusing – then, and ideally with the child, a short story is developed which brings into the story specific information about dealing with the situation. The story can be written down and illustrated with drawings or photographs.

The stories are developed using a balanced mixture of four elements:

- Descriptive statements that define and describe the situation.
- Perspective statements that explain the perspectives and reactions of people in that situation.
- Directive statements that guide what the child is to do or say that would be appropriate.
- Control statements that are strategies, based on the child's suggestions and can include ideas personalised to him, which help guide the child to remember what to do or how to act.

The stories are written in the first person and present tense for younger children or older children who may have specific language problems, but can be developed into other styles for older children. For instance, like a newspaper article. These stories can be effective because they help the child understand the context of the situation rather than directly telling a child how to behave in a situation where he may be confused, frightened or angry. The repetition that a story allows also helps the child learn. Although this technique requires appropriate training, the skills of the storyteller can enhance social story making.

opportunities for conflicts, arguments, reparations and resolutions are the classroom where much about relationships is learnt. Children often have painful, even traumatic, experiences that can affect their feelings of self worth and well-being. Being bullied or excluded from friendships are examples of this. Adults can help children develop important skills and stories are an excellent way of giving information that can be much more helpful than direct instruction which may be difficult for the child to carry out. Consider the difference between telling a child who has been bullied to 'ignore hurtful comments' and offering a story about someone in a similar experience. A story can help explore the emotional effects of bullying and suggest strategies that might be helpful. The listener can have the experience of being understood and to be given some choices about what to do. It may also give the person his or her own ideas about what to do. Stories can also be useful with working with children (and adults) who bully, they can help them learn about the consequences of their actions on others and increase their empathy with their victims. Educationalist and storyteller, Graham Langley, has written about using storytelling in tackling this issue.

Langley developed an anti-bullying intervention using storytelling, drama and discussion to explore the effects of bullying and learn conflict resolution techniques. Stories are used as a communal activity that makes it possible to explore bullying and the different emotions that are brought up by it. Storylines can engage and evoke strong emotions. By using stories, bullying could be explored at one step removed, creating distance, and the relationship with a storyteller can create an atmosphere of trust and safety. Asking children, in pairs, to describe an incident of bullying that they had observed, encouraged safe self-disclosure. Instead of directly saying 'this happened to me . . .' they had to turn it into a third person story. For instance, 'There was once a girl and what happened to her was . . .' This gave the tellers more control in being able to relate what happened. (5)

Amongst the key social skills and competencies that children need to learn and master to be able to enjoy successful friendships and relationships are:

- Learning social rules – how to act and behave appropriately in different social situations.

- Friendship skills – how to make and maintain friends, both in one to one and in groups.

- How to deal with conflicts with and between people – to know how to resolve conflicts and mediate in disputes.

- To know how to both praise and give negative feedback to others in a way that is helpful to the person.

It may be thought that it is not the role of schools to help children learn these critical skills and they will just learn them automatically. However, it is increasingly recognised that some children will need additional help in this area and that all children can benefit from learning more. There are many ways that stories can meaningfully contribute in this area. One project used animal stories to explore relationships between friends. The stories illustrated jealousies, loyalties and conflicts to help provoke thought about what it meant to be a good friend and to help think of alternative solutions to some of the problems raised by the stories. Another project for young people used stories about two friends that dealt with issues like sharing feelings with a close friend, having a trick played on you, how to help someone who is sad or depressed and of being bullied. Exploration of such stories can help with perspective taking and social problem solving skills.

Another application of using stories to build skills is the work of Keith Park with children and adults with multiple and severe learning difficulties. He uses call and response techniques to help engage listeners with the story. Using fairy stories, myths or stories from Shakespeare and Dickens, listeners become fully engaged and socially involved. Through gaining an understanding of the story, particularly concentrating on knowing what is on the other person's mind, social cognition and a 'theory of mind' understanding is increased (6).

One project used folk and fairy stories from the Brothers Grimm with adolescents with emotional and behavioural difficulties. Many of these traditional stories explore the transition from child to adult and many of the young people involved in this project were making this transition without a positive male figure in their lives who can act as a guide and were already disaffected from education. The folk stories were told to help develop listening skills and build trust in the facilitators. From this they were encouraged to share their own stories and using action games and role-play it became possible to explore their own beliefs about themselves and skills in relating to others (7).

So, stories can be used in multiple ways and on multiple levels to develop skills in the five pathways of emotional literacy. Stories are also used in many different ways in a number of therapeutic approaches, from speech therapy to psychotherapies, stories aid emotional and social skills. Of course it is not just the story by itself that does this; it is the interaction with the teller that turns the process of speaking and listening into a positive relationship that encourages growth. The teller can do much to facilitate the listeners learning by how they help the listeners discuss, reflect and think about the story.

Developing Reflective Thinking Skills

Stories are a particularly apt tool to develop emotional and social competencies in children because they enable us to talk about inner processes of thoughts, feelings, behaviours and relationships of the characters presented in stories. It becomes possible to talk about psychological issues without intruding into the private lives of children that will not always be appropriate. Listeners will often project their own meanings and interpretations and may disclose personal information when reflecting on a conversation and it will require sensitivity in setting boundaries around what is appropriate to talk about. Stories can be used through just the telling of the story alone without public discussion, or using them as a stimulus for debate, discussion and public reflection and also by helping children and young people create and tell their stories themselves.

Stories and narratives can allow us to talk about the feelings, thoughts, motivations and problem-solving strategies of the characters presented in the stories. To do so allows listeners to practise thinking skills around what they are hearing by reflecting on the story. These reflective thinking skills are key skills in emotional literacy and it is much safer for children (and adults) to explore these issues in stories than in exploring personal issues in the busy and sometimes chaotic atmosphere of the classroom. Exploring feelings in this way is much more 'natural' to how children learn to think about feelings. We learn to manage or 'process' feelings by being able to think about them. Children and young people can find it easier to think about feelings through the language of image and metaphor. By telling children stories it helps them to understand emotions without directly talking about their personal experiences, yet it gives them chance to make those connections themselves. Stories provide a language of the imagination and we can learn from these imaginative experiences. By talking about the emotional life we can help the child reflect on feelings and by using feeling words we build the emotional vocabulary.

Strong feelings can be difficult for children to manage and we often repress or deny feelings. Also, if we are talking about feelings in an attempt to manipulate behaviour (a common fault of adults) we will find there will be resistance in the listeners. So, any story that is used to evoke guilt, shame or humiliation is going to be counter-productive and would not be in the spirit of developing emotional literacy where the aim would be to transform emotions into adaptive responses. Children, like adults, will be aware if they are being told stories to manipulate them but may not be able to express why. Using stories to manipulate behaviour in an attempt to increase more acceptable behaviour should not be seen as a good outcome, and is likely to be counter-productive.

Using stories in Circle Time

It is important not to confuse teaching with learning. We can help children learn not just by imparting information, but also by using questions that help the child to think. Questions become a stimulus for enquiry and there will be times when it is appropriate to use questions that explore issues in the story and help stimulate debate. Telling stories in Circle Time is an obvious place where this would be appropriate and questions can be used either during the story or at the end. Robert Fisher has described in his book, 'Stories for Thinking' how stories and questions can be used to stimulate thinking skills particularly in critical thinking – thus laying down the ground for philosophical thinking (8). Such discussions can help children to:

- Gain confidence in raising their own questions and topics for discussion
- Develop their own ideas, views and theories
- Give reasons and explain their ideas to others
- Listen to and consider the views of others and to debate ideas and issues
- Change their ideas in the light of good evidence and reasoning – which develops a key emotional literacy skill, flexible thinking.

The aim is to create a 'community of enquiry' where people can learn together and from each other. Questions to guide discovery, often known as Socratic Questions, can be used to facilitate discussion. These are questions that often begin with, how, who or what. For example;

- "What do you think he meant by that?"
- "If that were true what would it mean?"
- Pick on a key word - "What does "wicked" mean?"

The teller can also comment on his or her own responses to the story itself as it goes along. This commentary of the teller's own emotional responses can help the listeners focus on their reactions to the story and facilitate the voicing of their thoughts (9).

Socratic questions can be used effectively with even very young children and they prepare the ground for higher order thinking. For instance, in exploring a story like the 'Emperor's New Suit' (see page 106) where everyone except some young children seem to be taken in with the belief that only the wise can see things that are not there, it might be possible to explore 'were people taken in by the idea the Emperor was wearing clothes that only the wise can see?', if so 'were they fooling themselves?', 'why was it only the young children who were not afraid to claim there were no clothes?', 'what might this story be about?' 'Is it telling us something about ourselves?' and so on.

Most stories make some reference to the emotions of the characters in the story or in the very least, convey an emotional tone be it suspense, happiness or sadness. This emotional content helps engagement in the story. The storyteller conveys emotion through the words and also through non-verbal communication. When there is a clear emotional message and the emotions conveyed are being described or labelled it helps extend or reinforce the emotional vocabulary of the listeners. This not only has the function of helping the listener understand and identify with the story, but it also helps their own emotional self-awareness. Young people vary enormously in the amount of emotional vocabulary they have, some will have a large vocabulary, others may be extremely limited. The teller's own emphasis in the telling, their own comments or the questions they ask, all can heighten the emotional content in the story. For example, the story of 'The Smuggler' (see page 102) was told to a group of Year Six children where a Customs Inspector was continually frustrated by not being able to find out how he was being tricked. The teller stops and asks the listeners, 'what do you think the Customs Inspector was feeling? 'Mad' shouts back one child. 'Wow, that's right. He was mad. Can you think of any other words that mean the same thing?' Calls of 'angry', 'frustrated', 'furious' and 'resentful' were shouted out. The teacher picked up on the word resentment and inquired further as to what it meant and why the character would be experiencing that. The class was asked as a whole what they thought was the best word that summed up the character's feelings. 'Angry' was decided upon and the teacher asked (introducing the idea of graduated strength in feeling) 'on a scale of one to ten, with one being a little bit miffed and ten being the most furious rage a person could ever feel, what number would you give him?' Various numbers were called out and the teacher took an average of the numbers and proceeded to tell what happened next, the children were intrigued to know what would happen next. It is extremely unusual for children to hear adults talk about feelings in this way but it is extremely helpful to them. Many children grow up not being allowed to be angry, and dealing with this emotion can be problematic for a large number of adults. How stories can be used to develop strategies for managing anger is described later. The teller could 'play' with the story – the class wanted the Customs Inspector to be really angry and the teller could make him so in the story. This improvisational skill calls on a willingness to play and to accept ideas that are presented.

Escaping into the Fantasy of Stories

Stories offer a way into an imaginative and fantastical world and often the question arises of whether this is a good thing or not. There is often a concern that a child can spend too much time in a fantasy world and may not be good at distinguishing between reality and fantasy. One way to help children be able to distinguish between fantasy and reality or to find the balance between them is to allow them to explore that fantasy world in company. For it is by being able to engage in fantasy that can make a child better able to deal with reality. A child uses his imagination not to escape from the real world but to be able to think about how it can be better.

Conclusion

A story, and the process of telling a story, evokes imaginative and creative thinking and emotion. This helps encourage engagement in the story. The fact that stories can mirror and reflect emotions and dilemma means they can safely point to new solutions or allow different perspectives to be seen. Stories might entertain and amuse, allowing humour to come into play or they might move, motivate and inspire. The exploration of a story can develop thinking skills but this does not mean they need always be rigorously interpreted. Sometimes, the story just needs to be told. Listeners will find their own meanings. As stories do not instruct they might circumvent resistance or blocks to motivation in learning. Stories and storytelling is, fundamentally, a safe container and medium for exploring the wider world and learning, as is illustrated in so many stories, that what appear insurmountable difficulties can be overcome.

Storytelling is more powerful than reading either to oneself or reading aloud because it happens in the relationship between speaker and listener. It is an act of communion that builds connections between people.

Notes

(1)   **'Bibliotherapy for Bereaved Children – Healing Reading'** by Eileen Jones (Jessica Kingsley Publishers, 2001)

(2)   **'The Bubblegum Guy'** by Joost Dorst (Sage/Lucky Duck 2004)

(3)   **'Life Choices'** by Phil Carradice (Sage/Lucky Duck, 2006)

(4)   **'The New Social Story Book'** by Carol Gray (Arlington/New Horizons, 2004)

(5)   **'Promoting Positive Behaviour - Activities for Preventing Bullying in Primary Schools'** by Jo Broadwood, Graham Langley and Helen Carmichael (Learning Design, London)

(6)   **'Interactive Storytelling'** by Keith Park (Speechmark, 2005)

(7)   **'Telling Tales to Promote Emotional Literacy'** by Steve Killick in Emotional Literacy Update, February 2006.

(8)   **'Stories for Thinking'** by Robert Fisher (Nash Pollock Publishing, 1996)

(9)   **'Classroom Tales - Using Storytelling to build emotional, social and academic skills across the primary curriculum'** by Jenny Fox Eades (Jessica Kingsley Publishing 2006).

Part Two

Why tell stories? In an increasingly speedy and technological world, an art form that was created by and continues to be owned by The People is indeed precious. Traditional stories leave no carbon footprint and have the potential to educate, enlighten and - through entertaining – de-stress the young and the young-at-heart. Storytelling is potentially a complete inter-generational activity. In an age where marketers have sought to create generational barriers through naming target groups - Teenagers, Toddlers or Old Folk – storytelling challenges this process: when sharing a story together, we're all just people. Something that is both simple and quite profound happens in a storytelling time. The essential components are a storyteller, a listener and a good tale. The teller and the listener bring something of their own life experience to the moment. Together they're both making the same journey. A warm relationship grows between the two through that storytelling moment. A good story well told has the potential to draw together a very disparate group of people, as this tale, gifted from my American storytelling friend Dan Keding, shows:

The Two Warriors

Two warriors faced each other, bloodied and bruised from their battle. Exhausted, they slumped to the ground, deciding to renew their fight the following day. Lying side by side as the light faded, they started to talk to each other. One produced a photograph of his son back home, who would one day become a soldier like his father. The other produced a photo of his daughter back home who would one day be a nurse, to care for wounded soldiers like them. The two enemies continued this way until the sun began to rise. Struggling to their feet, they sheathed their swords, embraced each other, and parted in opposite directions, for truly it is impossible for two people to hate each other when they know each other's story.

I am keen to present the potential of storytelling to enlighten in an unpretentious way. It is not necessary to conclude a tale with the clumsy "and the moral of the story is…"! Listeners, even the very young, have the ability to listen and decide what the story means for them. Even tiny infants, too young to understand a particular tale, can derive experience from the warmth of storytelling by sitting on the lap of or near a parent or peer, whilst everyone enjoys the shared experience.

The fact that an almost exceptional trust is quickly built between teller and listener is best illustrated by the following anecdote. Whilst telling stories to a small group of three and four year-olds in a north-eastern nursery, I was set back when a small boy stood up and pronounced, *"Oi, Storyteller, last night my dad gave my mum a black eye".* My first instinct was to feel relieved that nursery staff had witnessed this and could register the family had a problem of violence in the home. Secondly I felt it said something of the potency of the story session that it freed this troubled soul to unburden. I also felt a duty to register the unacceptability of violence in the home. So, I gently said, "That wasn't very good, was it?" The other listening children agreed, and pointed out that my story that had been interrupted was good and needed finishing. Both teller and listener quickly settled for the conclusion of the tale and peace and relaxation again filled the space.

The greatest threat to our tradition of storytelling is that we live in an age where most Europeans are time-poor. One Lakeland village, Staveley - which incidentally hosts a biannual storytelling weekend – had developed in an interesting way since the creation of a bypass. The road running through the middle of the village has now quietened to the point where locals and visitors alike can pause at the sides of the road, or even in the road, and just chat. It is this relaxed chat that gives birth to storytelling, for people remember their history as stories. Recently, telephoning Miss Rosa Hicks – the octogenarian widow of American mountain man and storytelling national treasure Ray Hicks – I mentioned that I understood since Ray's death she had started to tell stories. She replied, *"Not really, just talking on..."* and I realised that's all it is. Storytelling is as natural as breathing. Perhaps that's why it is relaxing and entertaining. The relationship between teller and listener is fostered by the subtle way the teller bends within the telling to satisfy the needs of the listener. This advances the ancient art above, for example, the television, which - despite all recent desperate attempts to make it interactive - once switched on, continues whether the person sitting in front of it is laughing, crying, or even dead! A couple more comments on the educational value of this art: there is no doubt that storytelling develops and fosters speaking and listening skills. It is possible to teach Geography by telling tales from distant lands, and equally lead into History; for example, some stories in this book – notably 'Trouble' (page 109) which, although given to me as a Jamaican story, originated in Africa and so almost certainly made that journey from one to the other via a slave. Thus an entertaining tale provides the perfect introduction to study history of the slave trade.

In a busy age it is debatable where the most appropriate venue for practising the art of storytelling might be. The answer has to be quite simply where people have the time to listen. There is currently an active storytelling revival of professional storytellers, many of whom prefer to practise their art in theatres and art centres, all places where the listener has to part with money to witness the art. Whilst I have no quarrel with this, being myself a professional storyteller, I favour the approach that the ideal home for the People's Art is wherever people meet together, i.e. in the community, in the home, workplace, or place of worship. Some of the stories in this book substantiate this approach; Death in a Nut (page 74) is regularly told for people dealing with bereavement - at home, in school or even as part of a funeral. If an art form is important then people will wish it to form part of their domestic rituals, whether they be births, namings, weddings or funerals. For family groupings, whatever the configuration, time spent sharing a tale will naturally lead to the opportunity to discuss other issues that may need confronting, e.g. bullying, stress etc... In sharing family stories and memories, there is a restatement by the participants of who and what they are. If all involved are happy with this, it is a boost to self-esteem, if not it will serve to name problems that can be dealt with, reference The Fearsome Giant (see page 66).

In an age when all generations are simply not taking sufficient exercise, a walk with stories may be the answer. If one of the party can come up with a story or a riddle for animals or objects spotted along the way, e.g. a bird or tree, the experience will be all the more rich and pleasurable. This probably begs the question as to whether everyone and anyone can tell a story. It is probably at this point worth saying that there is a world of difference from the role of a professional storyteller who like all performing artists, has to deliver the right story in the right way no matter how they feel on the day. Many of the finest storytellers do not even think of themselves as being 'storytellers'. To again repeat the words of Miss Rosa Hicks, they're "just talking on". To be inclusive and to enable anyone who wants to achieve some ability in the art for whatever reason, I describe the model of a practical storytelling workshop of about 1 hour, devised by myself and used effectively in schools, libraries, and for parents' and teachers' groups:

So You Want To Tell Stories?
The outline for a workshop created by Taffy Thomas, The storyteller

Note: this session is effective with a group of participants numbering between four and forty, but with an even number.

I usually start by convincing all present that they will leave having told a story. At this point some show signs of terror. Gentle questioning usually reveals the fear comes from a lack of trust in their memories and the lack of will to stand up in front of the group. I then reassure them that no-one will stand up in front of the group; they are merely going to choose a partner and swap stories one-to-one. In dealing with the memory fears, I point out that no-one has to remember any words because the nature of storytelling is such that the words can be different every time. I advise that the necessity is to develop a visual memory, a much-used technique in memory training. The participants are advised to visualise their brain divided into two halves. One half contains their vocabulary - as rich a collection of words and phrases as can be mustered (regional and dialect words are encouraged in this collection). The other half of the brain contains the story remembered as a series of pictures. All the storyteller does is to paint the pictures from one side of their brain, with words from the other side. This effectively communicates a picture from the teller to the listener. It is as simple and as complex as that! My favoured story to illustrate these skills and this technique is The Little Cobblestone Maker:

The Cobblestone Maker

There was a little Cobblestone Maker who was the finest Cobblestone Maker in the world. However, he was unhappy. Whenever he did his very best work, all people did was walk on it. He wanted to be more important, more powerful and stronger. He had some wishes. So one day he was chipping at a cobblestone wishing he was more important when there was a flash of light. He felt something heavy on his head and to his amazement, discovered he was wearing a crown, and a red cloak with white fur around the bottom.

All the folk in the street bowed and knelt down because he had changed into a king, and he thought,

'Great, now I'm important, now I'm powerful, now I'm strong. My wish has been granted. My ambition has been fulfilled.'

Just then the sun came out and all the people turned their heads to enjoy the sun, so he cursed. The sun is more important than a king so if I want to be the most important I must wish to be the sun. As he made his wish, there was a flash of blue light and he was up in the sky beaming down heat and light on the earth below, and he thought,

'Great, now I'm important, now I'm powerful, now I'm strong. My wish has been granted. My ambition has been fulfilled.'

Half an hour later a cloud passed in front of the sun, blocking out all the heat and the light. He cursed. A cloud is more important than the sun, so if I want to be the most important, I must wish to be a cloud. So he wished to be a thunder cloud, the strongest cloud of all. There was a flash of light and he was a liver-coloured cloud floating across the sky. All the people looked up. Seeing this dark cloud they ran for their umbrellas and raincoats. Just to make sure, he sent down a flash of lightning followed by a crash of thunder, followed by rain in torrents that washed the trees from people's gardens and sent a wild river racing down through the valley – a river in spate. The river crashed into a granite mountain, splitting into two streams, one each side of the mountain. Again he cursed. A mountain is more important than a flooded river, so if I want to be the most important, I must wish to be a granite mountain. As he made his wish, there was a flash of blue light, and he became a granite mountain standing four-square at the head of the valley. There he stayed as the days became weeks, the weeks became months and the months became years. One morning he woke with a tickling, itching on his back. He looked around and there on the back of the mountain chipping away patiently was . . . a little Cobblestone Maker.

So the little Cobblestone Maker realised he was important because we need people to make the roads. The one who cleans the hospitals is just as important as the one who does the operations. And the storyteller is just as important as the policeman, the teacher or the politician – but no more so.

The structure and shape and images of this story are so strong that all who hear it can recall what happens and in what order. The story also has a chorus or, as storytellers call it – a 'Run': 'Great, now I'm important, now I'm powerful, now I'm strong. My wish has been granted. My ambition has been fulfilled.' This happens every time the story moves forward to its next stage. It serves to give the tale shape, but more importantly allows the teller a moment's thinking time as they recite the 'run'.

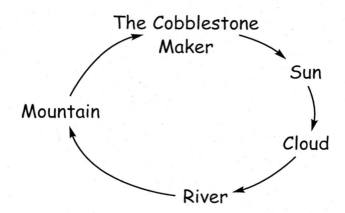

At this point participants are invited to choose a buddy to work with, either someone they trust or someone they're never likely to see again! One half of each pair retire to another space, leaving their buddies to hear a story. It is worth advising the listeners they need to be a good listener! I suggest 'Why Dog Lives With Man', again because of its shape and strong images:

Why Dog Lives With Man

Dog used to live on his own but Dog got lonely. He thought he needed a friend. Just then Dog spotted Hare. Dog thought that Hare could be his friend. Dog went over to Hare and said, "You and me could be friends".

Hare said, "OK, we'll give it a go".

In the daytime Dog and Hare went hunting together and at night they lay side by side. But in the middle of the night, Dog woke up and howled..."HOWWWWWWWWWL".

Hare said, "Don't do that. If you do that you'll wake up Wolf, and Wolf will come and kill us."

Dog reasoned that if Hare was frightened of Wolf, then Wolf must be the tougher. If this was the case then perhaps Dog should have Wolf as his friend.

Dog went over to Wolf and said, "Hey, you and me could be friends".

Wolf said, "OK, we'll give it a go".

So in the daytime Dog and Wolf went hunting together and at night they lay side by side. But in the middle of the night, Dog woke up and howled . . . "HOWWWWWWWWWL".

Wolf said, "Don't do that! If you do that you'll wake up Bear, and Bear will come and kill us."

Dog reasoned that if Wolf was frightened of Bear, then Bear must be the tougher. If this was the case then perhaps Dog should have Bear as his friend. Dog went over to Bear and said, "Hey, you and me could be friends".

Bear said, "OK, we'll give it a go".

So in the daytime Dog and Bear went hunting together and at night they lay side by side. But in the middle of the night, Dog woke up and howled . . . "HOWWWWWWWWL".

Bear said, "Don't do that! If you do that you'll wake up Man, and Man will come and kill us. Dog reasoned that if Bear was frightened of Man, then Man must be the tougher. If this was the case then perhaps Dog should have Man as his friend. Dog went over to Man and said, "Hey, you and me could be friends".

Man said, "OK, we'll give it a go".

So in the daytime Dog and Man went hunting together and at night they lay side by side. But in the middle of the night, Dog woke up and howled . . . "HOWWWWWWWWL".

Man said, "That's great! If you keep doing that you'll scare away Hare, Wolf, Bear, and burglars, and if you do that you can stay in my house and I'll feed you." And ever since that day Dog and Man have been the best of friends.

Their buddies return to the workshop space and are told the story by their partner. After the listeners have applauded the tellers, the tellers retire to another space, allowing their buddies to hear and absorb their story. I suggest 'Silly Jack':

Silly Jack

You probably know somebody like Jack. He wasn't all that bright and he wasn't all that fond of work but somehow he got by living on his wits. Now Jack wanted to be a farm worker. In those days, if you wanted a job on a farm, you didn't just go to the job centre, you went to the fair – a hiring fair. You stood in line and the farmer walked along inspecting his possible employees, feeling their muscles. He would then come to an agreement with them, maybe a shilling a week, for you could get a lot for a shilling in those days. They would then shake hands on the bargain.

Jack's mother sent him off to the fair, with the advice that farmers are very secretive about their financial affairs - a fact that is true even today - and that Jack, once he'd come to an agreement with the farmer, should keep it 'under his hat'. Jack stood in line and winced as the farmer squeezed his biceps, muttering something about 'knots in cotton'. However, Jack seemed fit and lively enough for employment, so the farmer took him on and they shook hands, agreeing a shilling a week. Feeling proud, Jack followed the farmer back to the farm and set to work with a will.

At the end of the first week, the farmer complimented Jack, presenting him with his first shilling. Jack knew he had to take this money home to his mother in gratitude for all the years she had looked after him before he found this, his first job. Thinking of his mother, Jack recalled her advice to keep all finances 'under his hat'. Jack balanced the shilling on his head and pulled his cap on top of it. He was so proud in becoming the provider that as he walked down the lane he leapt in the air, shouting, "WHOOPEE!" The coin slid off his head into a pile of mud and could not be found.

When Jack arrived home, his mother asked for the money. Sadly Jack explained what had happened. His mother looked him in the eye, saying, "You stupid, stupid boy. You should have put it in your pocket". Jack assured his mother he would try and do better the following week.

After a day's rest, when Jack and his mother relaxed together – neither mentioning the missing coin – Jack returned to his work at the farm. At the end of the following week the farmer again complimented Jack, telling him he'd done so well he was going to get not one shilling, but two. However, as the farm had a surplus of milk, the farmer was going to pay him two shillings-worth of milk. The farmer handed Jack the milk in a jug and Jack remembered his mother's advice to bring his wages home in his pocket. He tipped the milk into his pocket, it ran down his trouser-leg and out through the hole in his boot.

When he got home, his mother again asked for his wages and Jack sadly explained what had happened. His mother looked him in the eye, saying, "You stupid, stupid boy. You should have brought it home balanced on your head, like the women do in Africa".

After another day's rest, when neither Jack nor his mother mentioned the milk, Jack returned to the farm. At the end of that week the farmer told him he had again worked so well he would receive two shillings but this week there was a surplus of butter. Now these were the days when butter was slab butter. A large piece was cut off the side and wrapped in greaseproof paper – plastic had not been invented yet. Jack remembered his mother's advice to carry it home on his head. However, it was a hot summer's day. Before long the butter started to melt and Jack felt the grease running through his hair and down his neck.

When he arrived home his mother asked for the wages, and pointing to his greasy hair and collar, Jack explained what had happened. His mother looked him in the eye, saying, "You stupid, stupid boy. You should have wrapped it in leaves and carried it home in your hands".

The mother then complained she was a little lonely while Jack was away all week at the farm. When Jack returned to work, he told the farmer of his worries for his mother's loneliness. The farmer promised to try and help.

At the end of the week the farmer told Jack that his cat had kittens, and Jack could take one of the kittens as his wages to take home as company for his mother. Jack remembered he had to wrap it in leaves and carry it in his hands. The kitten didn't like this much and squealed, digging her sharp claws into Jack's hands. Jack dropped the kitten who shot off into a haystack and was never seen again.

When Jack arrived home he again had to explain this to his mother. His mother looked him in the eye, saying, "You stupid, stupid boy. You should have put a piece of string around its neck and led it home". She then told Jack that when he returned the following weekend it would be her birthday and she hoped he would earn enough for them to have a birthday meal together.

As soon as he arrived at the farm, Jack told the farmer about his mother's forthcoming birthday and the meal.

At the end of the working week the farmer gave him a leg of pork as his wages. Remembering his mother's advice, Jack put a piece of string around the leg of meat and led it down the lane behind him. A few metres down the lane, Jack heard the sound of yapping dogs. They snapped at the meat, so when he arrived home, all that remained was bone on a piece of string. Of course, Jack's mother said, "You stupid, stupid boy. You should have carried it home on your shoulders". Jack again apologised, for after all he was getting good at that, and told his mother he had one more week of his contract to work at the farm, and would try and do better. The following weekend the farmer paid Jack off, telling him he had worked so hard he would pay him something that would help him in the future. His wages would be a donkey, so he could start work as a delivery man, taking equipment from farm to farm and town to town. It was only then that Jack remembered his mother's advice and realised he had to carry the donkey home on his shoulders. He thanked the farmer, bidding him farewell. He ducked his head under the donkey's belly, and wrapped his arms around the donkey's legs. Struggling to stand up, Jack staggered down the lane, bearing the donkey on his shoulders.

On the way home, Jack had to pass the house of a very rich man. The rich man had a daughter who was melancholy – she never ever smiled. Her father said that if anyone could make his daughter smile they could have a million pounds, and the daughter's hand in marriage. It just so happened that as Jack was staggering past the house, the melancholy daughter was looking out of the window. She had often seen a man on a donkey but had never before seen a donkey on a man and she burst out laughing. Delighted, her father rushed to see the cause of the outburst. He summoned Jack into the mansion to give him his reward.

So that day Jack went home to his mother with a million pounds safely in a bag and a beautiful bride-to-be on his arm. His mother had to admit perhaps he wasn't such a stupid, stupid boy after all.

The other half of the group return to hear that story told by their buddies. The listeners of course applaud the tellers. At this point everyone in the group has told a story so the aims of the workshop have been accomplished.

As a professional storyteller I'm aware this is merely the start but, as Lau Tzu once said, *"All journeys begin with one step"*. I will take the time for some further advice to novice storytellers, advice that was useful to me as a novice some thirty years ago: firstly, take the story seriously, no matter how absurd the content or how full of inane repetition; if it is good enough to tell it should be treated with respect. On my first trip to perform in London in 1988, storytelling veteran Ben Haggerty greeted me at the station. Aware of my terror, he advised me to merely trust the story. I have subsequently come to learn that it is the story that is the star of any performance, not the storyteller, who is just a channel to pass on the tale. As twelve year-old Sarah Kennedy wrote, after enjoying my workshop at Keswick School,

> *A story's like a game of tig that's passed on*
> *And around. A story is like a gift that's*
> *Given by sound. A story is like a Mexican wave*
> *Whirling above the ground. Around and*
> *Around it goes, by word of mouth it flows*
> *Hold the gist as it goes by. Pass it on or it will*
> *Die. A story's a game of tig.*

If you can't feel respect for a particular story then choose another, because if you continue there will be a touch of shamefacedness in your telling that will transfer to the listener, breaking the spell. Take your time; there is a comfortable storytelling pace. This is not a licence to dawdle. If you adopt a business-like leisurely pace, there will always be time for a good tale. If you blunder, thanks to the tyranny of memory, the details are relatively unimportant, just pass right on. If the detail is crucial to the narrative, find a way of putting it in later as skilfully as you can - you can probably deceptively seem in the right order, rather than breaking the spell and the trust that exists between the listener and the teller. I was once asked on live radio the difference between a story and a joke. I replied that, "All good jokes are stories, but not all good stories are jokes". However, many good traditional stories, e.g. Jack tales, use humour to effect. For these there is value in the storyteller learning a little of the skills of timing employed by stand-up comedians. Whilst distancing ourselves from stand-up comedy, there is no harm in exploring the space between stand-up and storytelling. In such stories there is value in flagging up the approaching nonsense with a wry glance at the listener and "You're ahead of me, aren't you?" humour is often more potent building than surprising. In Silly Jack, the entire audience set up each piece of nonsense with the refrain, "You stupid, stupid boy". Everyone then further appreciates the pay-off when Jack gets the reward and proves that he isn't quite so stupid after all. Lastly, the pleasure of the teller will instantly communicate to the listener.

I am the luckiest man in the world: I enjoy telling stories to anyone who enjoys listening, always remembering that if speaking was more important than listening, we'd have two tongues and one ear!

Here's a last story, just for the love of the art:

The Pot of Dirt

The Mayor of the town was old; the time was approaching when he had to retire. His last job would be to choose a successor. Lots of people wanted that job, for you were driven round in a big car, for lots of free meals. There was one young boy called Jack who was desperate to be the new mayor. The old mayor had a problem; he was spoilt for choice, so he went to seek the advice of the wisest man in the town, Mr Merryweather, the Gardener. Together they came up with a cunning plan.

The following day all of the candidates lined up outside with their hands outstretched. On the end of the line was Jack. The mayor walked along the line, placing two sunflower seeds in each of their palms. He told them they must go home and plant the seeds in a pot. They must return in a month and whoever had grown the biggest and best sunflower would be the new mayor.

Jack ran home and found a large brown pot. He filled it with soil, made two holes with a stick, and planted the seeds. He pushed the pot out into the sunshine and rain, washed his hands and went to bed. The next morning Jack raced downstairs to his pot, looking for any tell-tale green shoots, but nothing grew. And so it was every day. All Jack had was a pot of dirt.

At the end of the month Jack's mother told him he should take the pot to the mayor's house and see if he had won. With a tear in his eye, Jack told her there was no point, as all he had was a pot of dirt. His mother told him he had to go as he had done his best.

Sadly, Jack took the pot to the mayor's house and stood in line with a tear trickling down his cheek. Ahead of him were people bearing pots burgeoning with enormous ripe yellow flowers. The mayor came out and gazed down the line, a line of enormous bright yellow flowers and on the end a tearful Jack with his pot of dirt. The mayor pointed to Jack, telling him that he would be the new mayor. Surprised, Jack reminded the mayor that there were loads of people with enormous flowers and all he had was a pot of dirt. The mayor told him that he had given everyone the same seeds, and before he had given them he had boiled them so they could never grow. So Jack was the only one who had been honest, and therefore the only one fit to be his successor.

Telling stories to children builds fundamental cognitive, social and emotional skills and helps them engage in the education process. But perhaps its most important contribution is that it lays the foundation for children to start creating and telling their own stories. They are learning fundamental speaking and listening skills that will help them be confident and competent communicators with resultant benefits for their well-being, behaviour and academic learning. Developing such skills is, of course, one of the essential aims of education, parenting and, indeed, all work with children and young people. Telling a story to others builds confidence and naturally develops language and communication skills. To be able to speak in front of others and sustain the interest of an audience helps a person feel competent. These skills help a person communicate the most important story they have, their own – the autobiographical narrative. The deepest purpose of telling stories is not to leave just stories in minds but to leave storytellers.

Teachers and those working in the areas of English, drama and the creative arts and PHSE will be particularly familiar with the processes involved in building these expressive skills. Building creative and imaginative thinking depends on facilitating relaxation and spontaneity and removing the anxiety of failure. Storytelling brings the perspective of building on visualisation skills and playing with words. There are many activities and exercises that teachers will be familiar with. In this chapter we present some ideas that practitioners may wish to incorporate into their practice. Some ideas can be used most effectively in one to one situations or small groups; others may be more use with classes and larger groups. Some exercises can be done in classes by breaking them up into smaller groups.

One key area to help children learn storytelling skills is about learning the basic sequence or structure of a story. The most basic structure is that of 'beginning', 'middle' and 'end'. The beginning establishes the setting. The middle is the main action of the story and the end is the resolution of the events. This basic structure involves putting things in order and linking events to each other that builds sophisticated communication skills.

When working with groups on creative and expressive activities it can be useful to set boundaries or ground rules for group members about what is and what is not acceptable. Establishing at the beginning boundaries such as respecting and listening to others can make it easier as it creates a climate within the group to be creative and imaginative. These guidelines can be discussed with the group, even inviting participants to decide on their own rules.

Creating a Storytelling Place

It can be useful to create a physical environment in which it is known that stories will be told. This might be done by creating a permanent space – a corner of the room for example, or by a ritual – for instance, placing a sheet over a chair or unrolling a special mat on the floor to signify it's story time. The group might be involved in the process. One class had a large table under which it was possible for a few children to sit. It was designated the storytelling tent and a sheet was thrown over it at break times. There, anyone could go to hear or tell a story. Another group made a series of small storytelling dens that were built for the activity then taken apart.

Many of the exercises here can be used to help build the storytelling skills and can be used either individually or in combination to create a storytelling lesson or workshop. It can be useful to combine some of the exercises here with those given in Part Two - Chapter 1 or to combine with the telling of some of the stories in Part One - Chapter 3. When doing so always be open to children or young people offering some of the stories that they know and have heard elsewhere. These have often been handed down in the oral tradition of their own family and this is a great opportunity for the stories to be retold and passed on.

Circle Games

Games that build mime and drama skills, besides being great fun, can aid visualisation and imagination skills as well. Ideal for groups up to about ten, they could be played in Circle Time although it may take some time to get round a whole class. These exercises also help develop the physical skills of storytelling and expressing emotion through body language. Such games are also very helpful in developing trust within the group and are good opportunities for learning interpersonal skills such as eye contact, turn-taking, negotiation and reciprocity.

The Invisible Box

An invisible box is passed around the circle. Each person opens it when it is passed to him or her and can imagine what they see in it. It may be something desirable, like a wished for birthday present, or something disgusting like a week old sandwich. The person decides what it is when they open the box and must demonstrate their reaction to whatever they see in the box. Afterwards they can say what it is they saw in the box or it can just be passed on.

Developments and variations

i) The item might be removed from the box and mimed giving other participants a chance to guess what it is.
ii) An actual box may be used instead of an imaginary one.

The Variable Ball

An imaginary ball is passed or thrown around the circle. It may start with the quality of a tennis ball but at the facilitators command it may change its nature to become a football, a ping-pong ball, a medicine ball and so on. As group members understand the game they may change the nature of the ball themselves.

Developments and variations

i)   Instead of a ball, any imagined item or object may be passed around that can change its nature at any time giving the opportunity to develop mime skills.

ii) A piece of used chewing gum (imaginary, of course) can be passed around the circle giving an opportunity to show expressions of complete disgust.

Killer (Wink-Murder)

This is a great game to develop eye-contact and emotional expression skills. The group stands in a circle with eyes closed. The facilitator chooses a 'Murderer' and 'Detective' by tapping once on the shoulder for 'murderer' and twice for the 'detective'. (Alternatively there may be some pre-made cards passed round with two cards marked accordingly). The Detective can declare himself but the Murderer remains unknown. On the command 'Let murder commence' the Murderer kills other members of the group by discreetly winking at them when, hopefully, no-one else will see. The person winked at waits for three seconds and then acts out a dramatic death.

The Detective has to guess who is the Murderer and has three guesses to do so. The Murderer's objective is to kill all the members of the group before being discovered or to evade being caught.

Developments and variations

At the beginning of each game a 'style' or emotion for dying may be decided upon such as 'angrily', 'suspiciously', 'joyously', 'quietly' and so on. Everybody has to die in this manner.

Lies, Damn Lies and No Statistics

Five Lies

This exercise, described by Phil Carradice (1) is about encouraging creative thinking by thinking about lies. We are all discouraged to lie and conditioned to see it as a bad thing, yet we must also learn there are times when it is important to hide one's feelings or be 'diplomatic'. In short, understand when not telling the truth is a necessary social skill. As many storytellers like to jest, storytelling is lying. This exercise gives the participant permission to tell lies.

Tell participants to write down the five biggest lies they can think of. Give some examples to give ideas.

"The world is not a globe at all – it is actually a giant Frisbee."

"I am third in line to become Queen of Ireland."

After people have written them down, go round in a group sharing one at a time. Not surprisingly, this exercise can generate a lot of laughter.

Catch Me Out

Divide a large group into groups of three. Each small group should share personal anecdotes of unusual things that have happened to them. It should only last about a minute. One personal story is selected for all members of the group to tell. Each member can personalise the story – i.e. change names, locations but not the key events of the story. Then, depending on the numbers in the group, one group can perform to the others. In larger groups, one group can 'challenge' another. Each person in the group tells the story as if it was their own. The audience then has to guess who the actual story really belonged to and can explore what led them to that conclusion. Some groups can be fascinated by this game and enjoy playing it for long periods of time.

Variations and developments

In groups up to ten a warm-up exercise can help develop this game. Participants stand in a circle and throw a ball to each other. Then one person can say something about themselves that can either be true or false but which is hard to tell e.g. "I have three brothers" or "I have been to India". They then throw the ball to someone else who has to decide whether the disclosure was true or false. That person then says something about herself and so on.

Visualisation

A storyteller does not tell a story word for word but draws upon the pictures they have in their imagination. With their words, the storyteller's goal is to paint pictures in the listener's mind that makes the story come alive. So visualisation is an important part of the storytelling process. Visualisation is also a foundation for creative thinking. Being relaxed is important for being able to visualise and for creative thinking generally. Often a solution will come to us when we are thinking of something else.

If we can visualise something in our 'mind's eye' we can begin to see beyond what is actually there. The ability to form a mental image can be developed. Indeed the words image and imagination share the same root. Such thinking then can be important for problem-solving and goal motivation, two important aspects of emotional literacy. Many people, including children have a tendency to visualise or imagine the future and can see it positively or negatively. We may 'catastrophise' and see the worst possible outcomes. For instance, to predict the poor results we will get in an exam and to see the looks of disappointment on everyone's faces. Such images can be anxiety provoking and de-motivating. However, we can change those images to be more positive to such things that will be more motivating – to imagine the feeling we will have when we succeed, to see and hear the applause after doing something extraordinary. Visualisation is an important part of building goal-setting skills as well as storytelling.

Our visual and language abilities work in tandem and exercises that use both sets of skills build on each other. Listening to stories helps develop these visualisation skills as the storyteller creates images that form in the mind. However, visualisation skills can also be developed through exercises that help build storytelling skills. Reflecting and talking about the images helps build the links between the verbal and non-verbal areas.

Guided Imagery Exercises

We visualise best when feeling relaxed, so cultivating this state of mind is the first step in creative thinking. Yet being able to relax oneself is an important life skill in its own right. It is worth spending time helping the group be able to relax perhaps by lying on the floor, focussing on their own breathing or listening to sounds in the environment. The tone of the facilitator's voice should be calm to help induce a state of relaxation into the room. Relaxation helps develop self-awareness and self-calming. When the group is sufficiently relaxed some of the following visualisation exercises can be used. Afterwards, participants may wish to share some of their experiences in pairs or writing and drawing exercises can be used.

- Imagine yourself lying in a deserted and beautiful place. It may be a beach or a glade in the woods. Perhaps it is at the top of a mountain. What can you see? What can you hear? What can you feel on your skin?

- Think of a meal you enjoyed. Can you see the food on the plate? Can you remember the taste? Can you smell the food as it was brought? Who else was there? What did you feel like when you had finished eating? (If the meal was enjoyed or the imagination was vivid it might not be surprising if such recall elicits some salivation.)

- Stories might be used as a stimulus. Part or the whole of a story may be told and particular focus put on such things as the landscape or on buildings and rooms in the story.

- With time, and if the group develops to be able to sustain such work, longer guided imagery exercises can be developed. For instance, as to imagine finding a house in the woods and to explore it, to enter into the perfect sweetshop and try different kinds of sweets or to imagine leaving your body and looking down upon yourself lying on the floor.

A Virtual Voyage around your Home

This exercise, adapted from one developed by Robin Moore (3) helps participants create vivid mental images. It takes about five minutes and needs a group in a calm, relaxed state where they can close their eyes. The facilitator gives the following instructions, leaving 10 to 20 second pauses between each instruction:

- "Close your eyes, sit (or lie) comfortably and imagine the front door of your house."

- "I would like you to imagine you are going to take a tour around your house. You will enter through the front door and go from room to room. Take your time and do not rush."

- "You will have about five minutes to tour your house. I will tell you when the time is up. Look at each room carefully and see all the things that are in that room, you will be able to spend a few moments in each room before slowly walking to the next room. When you have been to all the rooms come back to the front door and wait there."

- "Please open the door and start your journey. You have five minutes."

- (after four minutes), "You have one minute left."

- (one minute later), "If you are not already at the front door please move slowly towards it now."

- "Please leave your house and close the door. Bring your awareness back to this room and remember what this room looks like. When you are ready, open your eyes."

Impro Games

The games developed by Keith Johnstone (2) to develop improvisation skills build creativity, spontaneity and narrative skills. They can be used in small groups of about up to ten people including older children. Johnstone uses games and exercises to build improvisation skills and encourages people to be spontaneous by following some simple rules. These include such principles as:

- Aim to accept ideas rather than block them. We often block our imagination by not following the ideas we create. So saying 'yes' to ideas rather than 'no' helps spontaneity, creativity and imagination.

- One reason for blocking many ideas that come to mind is that we are often trying to be clever, original or funny and don't think our ideas are good enough. The search to be original is not the same as being creative and can slow the mind down as one selects some ideas and eliminates others.

- Anxiety may be one block to creativity in that we may fear that our ideas might reveal something about us or leads us into the unknown. The fear of failure of getting things wrong may also inhibit creative thought. Johnstone's approach puts an emphasis on how the mind can generate bizarre and unusual ideas quickly and spontaneously and the results of which are often very amusing.

- Becoming descriptive rather than moving the story on may also hinder story development.

Of course, generating spontaneity and creativity also involves complex social interactions and consideration of what is acceptable. Imagery can quickly become sexual, violent or challenging. Mature and secure groups may be able to cope with managing the boundaries about what is appropriate or not. There would need to be trust and security in the group to do so. However, this would not be appropriate for many groups and ground rules will need to be established about what is and what is not allowed.

One Word Story

Participants stand in a circle and by only saying one word each must build up a sentence. The first person to start a sentence should start with words such as 'I', 'Once' or 'The'. The next person follows with a word that makes grammatical sense that follows on from the first. It may take a group a few attempts to understand the process. The brain automatically generates words that it is expecting to hear (this is why we are able to understand what someone is saying to us as they speak rather than waiting till the end of the sentence). Saying the first word that comes into the mind enables sentences and stories to be generated quickly. If people are trying too hard to find the original or funny word they will slow the rhythm down.

It can be helpful to start just by working on short sentences and the facilitator may have to add punctuation or the sentences will continue without proper ending. When the skill of creating sentences has been mastered then one sentence can then be developed into a short story. Some of the stories will work, some will be non-sensical. Often they will be very amusing.

Storytelling Roulette

For groups of up to about ten. The participants stand in a circle and the facilitator is in the middle. The facilitator asks for suggestions for a location for a story and an object, perhaps an ordinary household object such as a 'frying pan' or 'tea-pot.' The location and object need to be woven into the story at some point.

The facilitator stands in the centre of the circle and points at one person. They have to tell a story for as long as the facilitator is pointing at them. Quickly and randomly the facilitator can turn and point at another person in the group and the person has to continue telling the story without pausing or hesitating. The facilitator moves quickly, keeping everybody on their toes as they may be called upon to continue the story at any point.

If the group is sufficiently comfortable and relaxed, an element of competition can be introduced. If anyone hesitates at any point in the story, they can drop out and the game becomes a competition to see who keeps telling the longest.

Story Challenge

In pairs, each child or young person has to think up some titles for stories and then challenge their partner to write the story. The story can be told or written down. The emphasis is on producing stories quickly and spontaneously and then developing the good ideas.

Story titles might be about social situations or conflicts that suggest the content.

> The Argument in Class
> The Day when Billy Kane got Rumbled
> The Assembly that Led to Disaster
> My Brother's Triumph

Variations and Developments

Instead of titles, the opening or last sentence of the story is given as the challenge. Alternatively, elements that have to be brought into the story can be given such as a location, a household item or even a relationship. One person might say to the other, "I challenge you to make up an instant story that includes a fish and chip shop and a vacuum cleaner." The other person has a few moments to think then starts to tell a story. The elements can either be significant or minor but must come in somehow. If the group get proficient at making instant stories they can try making instant poems.

The Storytelling Jacket

Get an old jacket or coat and put some items in the pockets. For instance, a train ticket, a letter, a book, a toy animal and so on. Give the jacket to a group to explore and discover the items. The facilitator asks questions to prompt imaginative responses from the participants.

> Who does this jacket belong to?
> What is in the pockets?
> I wonder why there is a ....?
> What do you think they were doing?
> Does this person have any friends?

The questions help build an idea of the jacket owner's life and from this a story can be developed either by the group as a whole or by individual participants.

The jacket and items may be very ordinary or they may follow a theme that is being covered in class. For instance, it might be clothing and items from a historical period that is being studied.

Six Piece Story-making

This method of helping children develop fairy tale like stories uses a simple structure based on common elements found in fairy tales. It is often used in therapy as an assessment tool and is described by Mooli Lahad (4) but can equally be used as a creative story making technique. It requires paper (A3 or larger) and pencils and crayons.

Participants are asked to tell a story without words, by scribbling and drawing the story in any way they wish. Ask them to listen to the questions and draw a picture for each question. They do not need to worry about the quality of the drawing as it is only to remind them what the story is.

Ask participants to divide the paper into six areas and to listen to the questions about the story. These are:

1. First Picture. Think of a main character for your story – a hero or heroine, he or she can be made-up by you, from a story or myth or from a film. Where does this character live? – a house, a castle – whatever you think. What is the landscape like?

2. Second Picture. In every story the central character has a task or mission or a problem to solve. What is the task for your character?

3. Third Picture. Is there anyone who helps the main character and how do they help?

4. Fourth Picture. Who or what is the obstacle that stands in the way of the leading character carrying out their task?

5. Fifth Picture. How will he or she deal with and try to overcome the obstacle or solve the problem?

6. Sixth Picture. What happened and what is the end of the story?

Participants then use each of the six areas to answer the six questions using drawings. It can be helpful to write the six questions up and to say how much time is available to draw the story.

When everybody has finished, participants then tell the story to either a partner, a small group or whole class, depending on the group's overall level of confidence in telling.

Variations and Developments

Sometimes part of a story may be told to help inspire imaginations and specific questions are then asked using the same structure of drawing pictures in six boxes. Some of the stories in Part Three might be suitable or the following story 'The Day the Fire Went Out' could be used.

Such exercises can be used to help assess a child's ability to sequence a story and the amount of emotional language and expression that is used as well.

The Day the Fire went Out

A long time ago, in a place far away, there was a deep forest underneath a mountain. Many were the animals that lived in the forest underneath the mountain. And in the deep, dark winter the animals gathered together in a clearing where there was always a fire to give light and give them warmth.

Great Bear was the one who always kept the fire going. He was strong, ferocious and brave. He had kept the fire going for so long that no one could remember when it had not been this way.

But one day Great Bear went into the deep, dark forest and did not come back. Eventually the fire went out. The animals got cold and they missed Great Bear but they also realised that they had to find a way to relight the fire and keep it going. Horse tried to light the fire but didn't know how. Elephant went to look for it but he couldn't find it anywhere. But maybe you know who did………

1. Who did find out how to restart the fire?
2. Who made the decision to find out?
3. Who helped?
4. What were the obstacles along the way?
5. How were they overcome?
6. What happened in the end?

Again, participants can tell their stories in pairs or to small groups.

Group Story

This is an exercise for helping a group compose a story and involves ways of making decisions together and needs small groups of about five to seven people. It can take between 30 to 45 minutes and some games can be played as a warm up exercise to this activity. The exercise involves asking the group to make a storyline for a film or video. It can be done purely as an imaginary exercise or as the start of a film or video project in which the film is actually made (although this may put some constraints on the content).

Firstly the group brainstorms ideas for things they would like to see in the film. This can include characters, locations and sequences. After a list is created, a discussion is opened about what ideas most excite the group. The group then has to enter a decision-making period of thinking about what it wants to include. The over-riding principle is to make sure everybody is included in the discussion. Voting for different elements could be included, for instance, everybody may have three votes for the bits they would most like to include, the most popular choices are included.

Once a number of priorities have been decided upon, the task is to turn them into a story that links the items. One group I worked with decided upon the TV cartoon characters, The Simpsons and wanted to include the Big Brother House and a fight scene. A story was developed of the Simpsons moving in the Big Brother House and having to live together for a week. They were given tasks to do and used the video diary to express how they were feeling as they got more frustrated with each other. Eventually it broke into a fight between Homer and Bart before they all realised they had to escape. The process of creating a story together as a group is the key task. This involves listening to each other's ideas and working together to solve the problems that arise.

The exercise can finish after they have developed a synopsis for the story that the groups can present or 'pitch' to each other. Alternatively, it can be developed into something that can be filmed or videoed. The above story involving the Simpsons developed after further discussion and thoughts about locations. It involved Bart Simpson meeting Darth Vader on a spaceship and discovering Darth Vader is actually his father, Homer. This was eventually filmed as a three-minute video story after ten weekly sessions. It involved the group thinking about story, characters, locations, learning stage-fighting and script writing skills.

NOTES

(1) **'The Write Way'** by Phil Carradice (Lucky Duck Publishing 1996)

(2) Keith Johnstone's books **'Impro'** and **'Impro for storytellers'** are great books not just for improvisational drama but also on human interactions.

(3) **'Awakening the Hidden Storyteller'** by Robin Moore (Shambhala Publications, 1991).

(4) **'Story making in assessment method for coping with stress - Six piece story making and BASIC Ph'** by Mooli Lahad. **'In Dramatherapy: Theory and Practice: Vol 2'** Edited by Sue Jennings (Routledge, 1992)

TELLING A STORY – Evaluation worksheet
After telling a story, ask yourself these questions...

Did you make good eye contact with some people when you were telling your story?

Did you remember everything or forget some parts? If you forgot any parts what did you do?

What do you think you did well?

Did you keep the audience interested in the story and what did they do that showed you they were or were not interested?

What could you do better next time?

What did you enjoy about other people telling stories?

Part Three

The stories contained here are a selection of mainly traditional tales for telling either one to one or to small groups. The stories are selected, not to overvalue these types of stories against other types of stories, but for three main reasons;

- These are good stories to learn if you are beginning to learn how to tell a story or wish to gain confidence in these skills

- They come mainly from an oral tradition and also are values-based stories

- These stories emphasise elements of emotional literacy and can be used to develop thinking in this area.

The collection begins with some riddles. Riddles, like jokes, aphorisms and proverbs, are a part of the foundation blocks of telling stories and are helpful in engaging listeners at the beginning or between stories.

Each story is followed by a brief commentary including the origins of the story, or at least what we know about it and where we heard it, and some thoughts about the themes of the story. These thoughts are intended to help stimulate ideas about how the stories may be used and the links with emotional literacy. However, it should not be seen as the only interpretation of the story, just a perspective. The meaning that the teller and the listeners find in the story as they experience and reflect on it is the most important.

Many of the stories included here come from Taffy's extensive repertoire of stories that, at the last count, was well over three hundred. Some of these stories, as far as we know, have not been written down before.

Riddles

The answers to the riddles are on page 120

I have an eye but I cannot see - what am I?

What is greater than God, worse than the devil? Rich men fear it but a poor man has it? Dead men eat it but if you eat it, you die – what is it?

The more you take the more you leave behind.

What is black when you buy it, red when you use it, grey when you throw it away?

A beggar had a brother who lived in Spain but the brother had no brother, please explain.

A wizard had seven daughters and each daughter had a brother – how many children did the wizard have?

I saw you where you never were, where you can never be. Yet, in that very place I saw you next to me.

Six arms have I, whole farms I can eat and a million of me can make a man – what am I?

Ten pull a woollen sack over a calf hill.

What is the question that can never be answered?

If two is company and three is a crowd, what is four and five?

Two coins make up 30p – one is not 20p – what are they?

How many times can you subtract 5 from 25?

I start with a T, end with T and am full of T – what am I?

A box without hinges, key or lid. Yet golden treasure inside is hid.

You go in of one and come out of three. But when you are out, you're in. What am I?

Before Mount Everest was discovered, what was the highest mountain in the world?

Thirty white horses on a red hill, first they champ, then they stand still.

I have a mouth but never talk. I can run but never walk. I cry but never weep. I have a bed but never sleep. What am I?

What do people make but no one can ever see?

What can you break with just one word?

What belongs to you that other people use much more than you do?

What has many holes but can hold water?

What has a spine and wears a jacket?

What is always before you but you cannot see it?

What has a head, a foot and ears, but no neck and no legs?

Two Legs put No Legs on Three Legs and went out. Four Legs came in and saw No Legs. Four Legs picked No Legs up and Two Legs came back in. Two Legs threw Three Legs at Four Legs who dropped No Legs and ran out. Two Legs put No Legs back on Three Legs. Who do the legs belong to?

Stories

The Blind Man and the Bird

Once a blind man lived in a cottage with his sister on the edge of a great forest. The sister started to go out with a man who was a bird-catcher. He used to trap wild birds, cage them and sell them in the market. The blind man became bored and asked the bird-catcher if he could go with him and help him with his work. Shocked, the bird-catcher said this would be impossible: the blind man would be walking into trees and more hindrance than help. The blind man explained that, although unsighted, his other senses were even more acute than usual. He would like to try.

On the following day the bird-catcher saddled a donkey and hung his bird traps around the saddle. He placed the blind man's hand on the back of the donkey and, taking the reins, started walking towards the forest. A short distance down a track, approaching a bend, the blind man screamed, "Stop! There's a lion round this bend waiting to pounce".

Cynically, the bird-catcher asked how he could ever know that. The blind man retorted that he could sense it. The two men and the donkey gingerly rounded the bend and, sure enough, there was a lion poised to pounce. From that moment the bird-catcher treated his companion with a new respect. They gave the lion a wide berth and carried on to a clearing in the forest. The bird-catcher set his traps, then, placing his hands on the blind man's hands, helped him to set a trap. The two men and the donkey headed home, knowing they must return the following day to check the traps. The following day they headed back into the forest, the bird-catcher leading the donkey and the donkey's broad back guiding the blind man. Arriving in the clearing, the bird-catcher discovered his traps had captured plain brown birds of little worth, although the one set by the blind man held a bright-coloured, valuable bird. The birds were taken from the traps and placed in individual cotton bags that hung around the donkey's saddle. On the walk home the bird-catcher crept behind the donkey and swapped one of his worthless birds for the valuable, coloured bird. He said to the blind man, "You tell me you're a wise man and I have reason to believe you. Then why is there so much war and hatred in the world?"

The blind man answered, "Because there are so many people like you in it, who help themselves to things that don't belong to them, and believe they have that right!"

Shamed, the bird-catcher slid back behind the donkey and swapped the birds back to their rightful places. As they approached the cottage, the bird-catcher said to the blind man, "You tell me you're a wise man and I have reason to believe you. Why is there so much love and joy in this world?"

The blind man answered, "Because there are so many people like you in it, who realise when they have done something wrong and are not too proud to put it right."

From that day, the bird-catcher, the blind man and the sister lived happily and with mutual respect in that cottage.

This story comes from Africa. It reflects a theme that emerges in many of the stories in this collection. That inside us there is the potential to act in different ways, positive and negative, good or evil, selfishly or with care and respect for others and we have a choice in how we act.

The Fearsome Giant

A long, long time ago in a far away land, there was a beautiful kingdom nestled in a peaceful valley surrounded by towering mountains.

There was only one road into the valley, it was the only way to enter or leave the kingdom. The road passed between the two massive mountains through a gap created by the waters of a bubbling mountain stream. It was a very busy road and often filled with people merrily coming and going. People would come from far and wide to visit this peaceful kingdom.

All seemed well.

One day something terrible happened. At the border of the kingdom, at the side of the one and only road into the kingdom between the two mountains, a fierce and Fearsome Giant came to live. Stories spread quickly claiming that the Giant frightened all the people coming and going along that road through the mountain gap. It was said that Giant would stand and cast his long shadow across the land and the Fearsome Giant's voice would thunder,

"Swish, swash, thump, boom.
I am your nightmare.
I am your doom!"

The people ran away frightened and they would tell tales of terrible things the Fearsome Giant did, how he smashed a wagon by throwing a boulder at it or he would jump up and down and make the Earth tremble for miles around and all the time chanting,

"Swish, swash, thump, boom.
I am your nightmare.
I am your doom!"

The people were so frightened they decided to go to the King and say that something must be done. Now, the King of this land was a young man, a very young man indeed. In fact, he was still a boy who had only recently become King. His parents had been King and Queen for a very long time. They had been very wise and were much loved by the people but they had died just before the Fearsome Giant had appeared. The young King wanted to prove himself as brave and wise as his parents but he secretly feared that he just wasn't good enough.

"You must send out the Knights!" the people demanded of the King. "They must destroy the Giant." The boy was young and uncertain so thought he must do as the people demanded as that should make them happy. So the King called his four bravest Knights. These Knights were so brave, they were possibly the bravest Knights in the whole world and they could always manage every problem. The King was certain they could deal with the Giant. He commanded the Knights, "Go forth and drive the Fearsome Giant from our land." The people applauded and cheered as the Knights set out; they were filled with pride and hope.

Although they were very brave and capable, as the Knights became close to where the Giant lived they started to get worried. They told each other the terrible stories they had heard about the Giant and as they realised that none of them had faced a Giant such as this before their confidence crumbled and they were afraid.

As they reached the mountain gap, the Giant rose to his feet and stood before them. He cast his long shadow across the Knights and then jumped up and down. The Earth trembled mightily and then his voice thundered,

"Swish, swash, thump, boom.
I am your nightmare.
I am your doom!"

The horses reared up on their hind legs, dumped the Knights on the road and galloped away with the Knights running behind them.

Well, if the people had been scared before, when they saw that the Knights had failed, they were terrified. They demanded that the King do something about the fierce and terrible Giant. The young King did not know what to do; he wished his father and mother were there because they would know what to do. He missed them very much.

But then he remembered the wise old hen-wife. She lived at the edge of town and raised chickens. He remembered that his mother trusted her and he heard people say how much she had helped them. He had never met her and was a bit nervous about going to see her but he decided he had to be brave and ask for her advice.

The young King found the hen-wife in her cottage surrounded by chickens. She was sitting in a rocking-chair, knitting. She was very old but the young King could see her wisdom. She had a very warm smile.

The hen-wife invited the young King into the cottage and offered him a cup of tea. Immediately the King felt comfortable with her. The hen-wife asked how she could help the King. The King told her all about the Fearsome Giant and the terrible stories he had heard. The hen-wife listened carefully and when the King had finished speaking she thought for a long time before speaking, but finally she spoke and said,

"We run from what we do not know,
and then it seems to grow and grow,
and then it stands within our way,
Until its name we learn to say."

And then the hen-wife smiled and returned to her knitting.

As you might imagine, the young King felt a bit confused. He left the cottage of the hen-wife and returned to the castle. He thought and thought about the riddle but still didn't know what to do. He had wanted her to tell him what to do but it seemed that she had wanted him to figure it out for himself. But he certainly felt better for having spoken to her.

The people were still calling out for the young King to do something, even the so-called brave Knights. What was he going to do? He was frightened just thinking about the Giant but he knew he had to be the one who sorted it out, that's what kings do. Everyone was depending on him. Then he thought about the riddle of the wise old hen-wife.

"We run from what we do not know,
and then it seems to grow and grow,
and then it stands within our way,
Until its name we learn to say."

The young King made a decision. He spoke to his people and told them he would face the Giant and they all stared on in disbelief as they watched him mount the royal pony and begin his journey to the dangerous border.

As the young King approached the border, the fierce Giant stood up and towered over him. The Giant gnashed his teeth and growled loudly. The young King was scared, very scared. His royal pony was scared. So scared, that the King had trouble controlling him.

The King dismounted and tried to tie his pony to a fence but the pony raced away towards the town. The young King stood all alone before the huge and terrible Giant.

The Giant jumped up and down and the Earth trembled. The Giant's voice thundered,

"Swish, swash, thump, boom.
I am your nightmare.
I am your doom!"

The young King felt a very large knot in his stomach and his legs were feeling like jelly. He was scared. The trembling of the Earth and the roaring of the Giant caused the young King to take several steps backward. But as he took each step backward the Giant seemed to get bigger and bigger.

The young King was terrified. He wanted to turn and run away from the huge and horrible Giant. But he also wanted to do what a King must do, whatever that was. He stopped himself from running. He took a deep breath and had a long think. He realised that the Giant was only shouting and actually wasn't doing anything to harm him. Then he remembered the riddle of the hen-wife,

"We run from what we do not know,
and then it seems to grow and grow,
and then it stands within our way,
Until its name we learn to say."

Then the King understood. He realised he must learn the name to call the Giant. He decided to face the Giant, not knowing what would happen and took three steps towards the Giant.   As he took the steps, a strange thing happened. The Giant seemed to get smaller.

This was a surprise, so even though he wanted to run away, he decided to keep on walking towards the Giant. With each new step the Giant became smaller and smaller in size. The Giant jumped up and down but the Earth had stopped trembling. He tried to roar but what came out was just a squeak and not like thunder at all,

"Swish, swash, thump, boom.
I am your nightmare.
I am your doom!"

The young King kept on walking right up the Giant and saw that he was no bigger than his thumb. The King bent down and picked up the tiny Giant and stood him on the palm of his hand.

He wondered how the Giant could have done all the things the people said he'd done.

The King looked him in the eye and asked, "What is your name?"

The tiny Giant blinked and proclaimed,

"My name is FEAR."

This story, which is believed to come from Wales, is a wonderful story about facing up to fear and reveals much about the nature of anxiety and worry. The metaphor of a giant who grows bigger the more he is feared but is defeated when confronted is a powerful way of communicating to people how fears can be overcome by facing rather than avoiding them. The boy has to do this for himself and there is no one else to do it for him.

The story clearly describes the experience of an emotion, and it is very easy to underestimate just how useful this is for children in learning about the experience of feelings. The young boy is described as having a 'large knot in the centre of his stomach and his legs were feeling like jelly' and this feeling is labelled as being 'scared'. Such descriptions greatly aid the development of an emotional vocabulary and understanding of the emotion. Many people are not aware that these strong physical effects are emotional and may believe that they are physical problems that might contribute to psychosomatic difficulties or make it harder for them to feel their worries.

Even if we do not know what it is like to face a giant, we do know what it is like to feel worried and scared and the message that it can be overcome is therefore an optimistic one. The young child facing anxiety may often search out the adult carer in his life with whom he feels most secure. However, the boy in this story has lost his loving parents who would have been his secure base, yet this is not a story that focuses on this loss. One view may be that this story is about growing up and becoming autonomous and that the death of the parents is just a metaphor of this as the child learns that he is able to do things for himself.

The Wolves Inside

A young boy was spending time with his grandfather. One day he asked him, "When I grow up, what kind of man will I be?"

"What do you mean?" asked his grandfather.

"Well, I want to know if I will be good or bad," said the boy.

"I don't know. It depends," said the grandfather.

"Depends on what?" said the boy.

"Well, inside of each of us are two wolves and sooner or later they have to fight with each other. One of the wolves fights for hope and kindness. The other wolf fights for selfishness and anger. What kind of man you will grow up to be will depend on who wins the fight, whether it is the Good Wolf or the Bad Wolf."

The boy looked alarmed and asked, "How will I know which one will win? Is there nothing I can do?"

"Ahh," said the old man, "the one that will win will be . . . the one that you feed."

This short and enigmatic story, which we believe to be an old Native American story, reflects a universal theme. The internal battle inside between being full of love and compassion or consumed by anger and hate is described in the metaphor of two fighting wolves, the good wolf and the bad wolf. It also suggests that the victor will be the one that is encouraged or 'fed'. Anger and hatred can indeed consume us and override other aspects of our personality if we dwell on it and feed it through our thoughts. To deal with feelings such as anger, sometimes we have to let go of them, to give up our resentments and search for understanding of those we feel have wronged us. This story acknowledges the control we have in that eternal struggle through choosing which parts of ourself that we wish to nourish.

The Three Friends

In the days when the counties of Cumberland and Dumfries were the debatable lands - meaning that the position of the border between England and Scotland was variable - the northern affairs of Good Queen Bess (Elizabeth I) were administered from Carlisle Castle by one Lord Scrope. Now Lord Scrope was hated by the Scots because he was English, and hated by the Carlisle folk because, when their families were starving, he had come from the south to take the only decent job.

One night Scrope was in bed in the tiny room above the castle archway - that can still be visited to this day - when he heard the sounds of someone breaking and entering. Scrope called for his guards and who should they find but Willie Armstrong, know as Kinmont Willie, leader of the notorious border 'reiver' clan, the Armstrongs. Scrope asked Kinmont Willie what he was doing creeping in at dead of night without invitation. With something between honesty, bravado and stupidity, Willie retorted that he had come to murder Scrope. Scrope ordered his guards to chain Kinmont Willie, telling him that in the morning he would be hanged. The Lord then got a response he hadn't expected. Willie requested not to be hanged in the morning but to be hanged in two days time. The Lord queried this strange request and Willie told him that very morning he needed to attend the wedding of his cousin Johnny Armstrong, and act as best man. Lord Scrope spotted trickery afoot and thought that if he released Willie for the wedding he would use it as a means of escape and not return to be hanged! Willie asked if he could provide a friend to stand in his stead in the cells who would be hanged should Kinmont Willie fail to return by the appointed time. Scrope asked if he had such a friend. Willie replied that his best friend, Jamie Bell, would stand in his place.

Jamie Bell was summoned to the castle, and Scrope explained to him that he would be imprisoned in the dungeons in the place of his friend Willie, and should Willie fail to return by noon, two days hence, then he would be hanged by the neck until dead. Jamie nodded in agreement confidently announcing that his dear friend Kinmont Willie would keep his promise and return in time to save his neck. Lord Scrope looked on in blank astonishment... Jamie was led down to the dungeons in chains and Willie Armstrong told he was free to go to attend the wedding of his cousin Johnny Armstrong.

Kinmont Willie was best man at his cousin's wedding and enjoyed the celebration that followed, where the tables were groaning with food and drink. Willie consumed so much wine and whisky that the following morning he overslept. Waking late with a thick head, he remembered he had to make it back to Carlisle by noon or his best friend Jamie would be hanged! With a quick goodbye to the rest of his clan, he leapt on his horse and started to ride like the wind. Galloping round a bend, he spotted a mixed gang of the Grahams and the Kerrs under a tree, waiting to ambush him. Willie leapt from his horse, drew his sword and his dagger and set about them. After an hour's stabbing, bruising and battering, there was a pile of the corpses of the Grahams and the Kerrs. Despite being exhausted and spattered with blood and gore, Willie knew he had not a moment to waste. He struggled back on his horse and continued his race against time.

A little further down the road, Willie arrived at the river. The water was in flood and Willie knew that it contained eels with needle-like teeth. However, he had no choice but to struggle across it. He gripped his dagger in his teeth, dived into the torrent and struck out for the far shore. Every time an eel neared him, he stuck his dagger in the top of its head. By the time he crawled out on the far shore, the river was a mass of dead eels, floating white belly-up. Willie was now covered in a mixture of blood, and eel-slime. He realised he had less than an hour to cover the last five miles to Carlisle Castle. He staggered up the road despite his exhaustion running where he could, and made it to the castle gates a couple of minutes before noon.

Two guards stood in front of the gate. Peering over their heads, Willie saw the gallows had been built in the Castle Square. His best friend Jamie Bell was stood on the trapdoor with a noose around his neck. The executioner's hand was on the lever and twitching. Willie had to do something quick. With the last strength he could muster, Willie knocked out the guards with two wild punches. He leapt over their bodies and ran into the square, screaming, "STOP, STOP!" He told the executioner he was about to hang the wrong man and that it was indeed himself that was supposed to be executed. The hangman looked helplessly at Lord Scrope, who was there to witness the execution, and asked which man he was to hang. Scrope announced that Willie and Jamie were to be imprisoned in the dungeon for one last night whilst he decided which one was to die. Kinmont Willie and Jamie Bell were shackled and led down to the cells, for what was to be an uneasy night. With the first light of morning, Willie and Jamie were led into the square to face Lord Scrope and the noose. Lord Scrope told them he had been considering it all night, and then pronounced . . .

"If I let you both go free, could I be the third friend?"

A story from the 'debatable lands' where the feuding families were known as 'reivers' because they made their way by robbing and thieving. This became 'reiving'. Incidentally it is from this word that we now have the word bereaved, for if a reiver gang raided your house it was likely someone would be killed and the family left 'bereaved'. The story raises the theme of the loyalty of friendship.

Death in a Nut

Jack is the hero of many folk tales. We all know a Jack. He isn't that bright, he's not over fond of work, but somehow he gets by living on his wits.

Now Jack at the time of this story lived with his mother. They were very poor. However they lived by the seaside and just about got by, providing that every day Jack went down to comb the beach, looking for things that had been dropped or thrown from a passing ship or boat. These finds could either be swapped for food or sold to make money for food. Jack and his mother were not the only poor people in that community, so many were beachcombers; if Jack wanted the richest pickings, he would have to go down for the earliest tide. No matter what time Jack set off in the morning he always took his mother a cup of tea in bed, for there is no finer thing a child can do for their mother than to take them a cup of tea in bed in the morning!

One early morning Jack took his mother a cup of tea in bed and to his distress she was as white as the pillow she was lying on. He asked if she was poorly and she told him she was very sick and this would be the day that 'He' would be coming for her. Jack's eyes filled with tears for he knew his mother was telling him it was the day 'Death' would come for her. Proudly he announced he would see to it that 'He' didn't take her. He put the cup to her quivering lips. Tenderly, he leaned forward, kissing her cold cheek, knowing this might be the last time he saw his mother. He kissed her again and drew away from the bed and out of the room. He returned the cup to the kitchen and with tears running down his cheeks he went out of the back door.

He climbed on his bicycle and pedalled down to the beach. He tossed his bike down on the pebbles and started to comb the beach for any valuable objects. In the distance Jack could see a stranger trudging towards him. The stranger had a head like a skull with two black eyeholes and a long, black, hooded cape. Over his shoulder was a brand, spanking new scythe, the blade gleaming in the early morning sunshine. The stranger trudged up to Jack and asked if he knew the way to Jack's mother's cottage. Defiantly, Jack faced him and shouted, "I know who you are and what you've come for and you're not having her". He seized the scythe and smashed the pole across his knee. Wielding one half of the pole, he bashed the stranger over the head. He smote him blow after blow until the stranger was no bigger than his thumb. Looking down between his feet, Jack spotted a nutshell. It was a hazelnut that some squirrel had eaten the middle from, leaving the shell with a hole. Jack stooped and picked up the shell, he seized the shrunken man and forced him into the shell using a piece of stick to plug the hole. Triumphantly, Jack tossed the shell out into the tide, watching it bob around several metres from the shore. Jack continued on his way, finding one or two useful pieces of flotsam and jetsam. Job done, he turned on his heel and made his way back home.

As Jack walked up the lane to Rose Cottage, he could hear the sound of singing and merriment coming from the kitchen. Surprised but happy, Jack opened the back door to see his mother singing and dancing around the kitchen with a broom. He told his mum that he thought she was so sick that she was dying. She retorted that something very strange had happened, as half an hour before his return she had started to feel like a young girl again. In fact, she told him, she felt so good that if he would like to go to the butchers and buy some bacon, she would cook him his favourite breakfast of bacon and eggs.

Now Jack delighted in a cooked breakfast, and was so pleased to see his mother fit and well that he skipped out of the kitchen, leapt on his bike and pedalled off to the butcher's shop. The butcher stood in his bloodstained apron in the shop doorway sharpening his blade. Jack greeted the butcher like an old friend and asked for a pound of best back bacon. Angrily the butcher told Jack he had no meat to sell that day, as there was something very strange abroad in the world. On arriving for work that morning the butcher had several animals to kill, but nothing would die. He had tried to cut the pig's throat but no sooner had he wielded the knife blade than the cut healed up. Now Jack by this time was feeling a little shifty, suspecting that the 'something' that was abroad in the world might be connected to his activities on the beach early that morning. He wished the butcher well, telling him he was going to take a turnip from Farmer Merryweather's field on the way home, commenting that turnip and eggs would now be his favourite breakfast.

Climbing on his bike, Jack thoughtfully cycled to Farmer Merryweather's field. Wriggling through the hedge he seized hold of a turnip and started to tug. Now Jack was a fit, strong lad of some seventeen or eighteen years but no matter how hard he tugged and twisted and pulled, the turnip would not let go of the ground. Frustrated, Jack gave up and cycled home. When he arrived in the kitchen it was full of smoke and his mother was muttering. She asked if Jack had bought the bacon, and he told her that the butcher had no meat to sell, as nothing would die. There was 'something' very strange abroad in the world!

His mother agreed that there was something strange as she tried to light the fire with fine dry kindling and all it would do was spit and smoke. Furthermore, she had tried to crack some eggs into a bowl ready for the scrambled eggs but the shells had proved unbreakable.

Now Jack was not the sort of son to lie to his mother, either through untruths or lying by omission, and he had a shrewd idea that his actions were not unconnected to all that was going wrong. He described to his mother all that had happened on the beach that morning with the stranger, the scythe and the nutshell. Just as he feared, his mother was thrown into a rage, telling him he was stupid and that he alone had destroyed 'Death'. Jack said that was exactly what he had intended as he wanted to protect her. She told him that he had robbed her of her moment, for just as there is a time to be born into this world, there is a time to leave it, and without Death there would be no new animals, no new plants, and no new ideas. Apart from that she had told him all of her wonderful stories and it was for him now to make his own way in the world, armed with his mother's tales and teachings.

Jack apologised, saying that it now occurred to him that Death was an important part of life. He begged his mother to tell him what he could do to put things right. She told him that all he could do was to go down to the beach, release Death from the nutshell and make his peace with him. Jack hugged his mother again, saying sorry, and running out of the house, he jumped on his bike and pedalled back to the beach. Leaving his bike down on the pebbles, he was delighted to spot the nutshell bobbing around in the waves. Rolling his trousers up Jack waded in and, stretching out his hand, seized the nut. Carefully he carried it back to the shore and pulled out the wooden plug.

The shrunken man drew himself back up to his full height and stared eyeball to eyeball at Jack: "You broke my new scythe". Shaking, Jack apologised, telling the man he had no idea he was an important part of life, but that if the old man sat down on the beach, he would do what he could to put things right. Jack found a new piece of wood and hammered the scythe blade onto it. He set the repaired scythe on the old man's shoulder, again apologising profusely. The old man asked him again the directions to Jack's mother's cottage. A little wiser, Jack told him to turn right, left and right again and that Rose Cottage was on the right. He pleaded with the old man to be very gentle with his mother and the two parted. The man went trudging along towards Rose Cottage and Jack had one last look along the beach. As he did this, Jack saw the sun, the sea and the sky with beauty he had never noticed before. After collecting one or two things, Jack turned again, making his own way home.

As Jack went up the garden path, this time the kitchen and the house were in complete silence. Opening the back door, Jack knew exactly where his mother would be and hurried to her bedroom. As he expected, his mother was lying on the bed, completely still with a smile on her face . . . but dead.

Jack called a few friends together and they had a party telling all of

Jack's mother's stories and remembering all of the good times they had had with Jack and his mother. In fact they even got to laughing about some of the bad times as well. Then they took his mother's body and buried it in a hole in the ground from which she had come, and drank a toast to her memory. Jack walked back through the kitchen, picking up a bag of gold coins from the shelf that his mother had saved for a rainy day. Armed with that, and the stories and teachings from his mother, he set out to make his own way in the world, where he had many more adventures - but they are other stories for another day . . .

This story was gifted to Taffy by his friend and mentor, Duncan Williamson, a Scottish Traveller and renowned storyteller. The subject matter of the story centres upon death, particularly the impending death of a parent. Jack finds that death cannot be prevented and to do so disrupts the cycle of death and renewal and he learns that death is an important part of life. In so doing he has been able to grow up and become an independent adult himself.

Many children will have experienced the loss of a loved one in their family, perhaps even a parent. The effect of such a loss can never be predicted, but for many it will be a time of uncertainty and change on top of trying to deal with the complex feelings of grief, the mourning for a loss of a significant person. School offers structure and continuity, but it can be difficult for others to know how to help as it can be hard to know what to say, sometimes nothing gets said. From this, a cycle of silence develops. Education about death and loss is seen by many as an important part of education. Stories offer a way of examining, at a distance, the process and sometimes very painful feelings of loss.

Field Of Gold

Far away on a remote island, a peasant farmer lived alone with his three sons. Together they worked a patch of land the size of a pocket handkerchief, although it should be noted the three lads showed more interest in lying in the sun and swimming.

Realising he was in the autumn of his years, the old man started to fear for his sons' future. He sat them by him and, pointing, told them there was gold in that field. The boys looked surprised and asked him to explain. He told them that when their mother was still alive, the two of them placed the gold they had saved into a pot and buried it somewhere in that field. The three lads muttered disconsolately, believing their father to be stupid, for he had in no way identified the site of the burial.

Some months later the old man peacefully died. For the days and weeks following, the three brothers spent what little money was left in the cupboard and ate what little food was left in the larder. The following week the brothers started to feel the pangs of poverty and hunger. Then the oldest brother remembered their father had told them about the gold in the field. The three brothers had no option but to put on their boots, go out to the field and start digging. With no real system they searched without success and dug up the whole of the field. Collapsing in exhaustion, they ruminated on the stupidity of their late father.

The older brother, realising the field had been completely turned over, thought the only stupidity would be if their work were wasted. With this in mind he went to market and bought a cartful of young banana trees. Together the three brothers planted those trees in rows, in the field they had inadvertently dug over.

Nature, the sun and the rain, did their work and the trees grew big and strong and covered in bunches of green fruit. With the island sunshine, the fruit ripened to a bright golden yellow. The brothers harvested the bananas and sold them at market. Returning with their pockets jingling with gold from their sales, they mused that perhaps their father hadn't been quite so stupid, for there had indeed been gold in that field.

This story reminds us that we have enough to survive in our immediate environment, indeed it is our greatest wealth although it may need work and effort to reap the rewards. A similar outlook exists in a version of the proverb, "the grass always looks greener on the other side of the fence". This proverb has a less well-known rejoinder, "if the grass always looks greener on the other side of the fence, then maybe you aren't tending your own patch enough".

The Cracked Pot

It was hot, it was dusty and the old man was grateful for the two pots he used to carry water up from the river to his house. He had had them a long time. One was perfect and beautiful to look at but the other one was cracked. The old man had filled them both to the brim at the river bank, but by the time he had walked back to the village the cracked one was half empty and the perfect one was still full to overflowing.

Now the perfect pot became very proud. "I'm much better than you," he boasted to his companion, "I don't know why he doesn't just smash you and get another beautiful pot to keep me company. You're not very much use, are you?"

The perfect pot went on and on like this every day, so much so that, eventually, the cracked pot felt so sad and useless that he went to the old man and said to him, "I'm not very much use to you. I've leaked half my load by the time you've come back from the river; you really ought to replace me with a new pot, then you won't have to make so many journeys."

"Oh no," said the old man, "look down the path to the river. What do you see on the side that I always carry you? Lots and lots of beautiful fragrant flowers. Without you they would never grow. You've brought colour, beauty and fragrance into my life. I could never replace you when you've enriched my life a thousand-fold and that of the other villagers. A new perfect pot could never do that."

Versions of this tale have been found in India and China and sometimes it is an old man, other times an old woman. But its message is clear, it is our flaws and cracks that makes us who we are and life is enriched with beauty by our uniqueness, not by perfection. So take a deep breath and smell the flowers, because who do you know that hasn't got some cracks somewhere?

A Man and a Dog

A man and his dog and were walking happily together along a country road. The man was enjoying the beautiful views when suddenly he remembered something. He remembered he was dead. His last memory was of him closing his eyes and dying. He turned and looked at his dog and remembered that his dog had died many years ago. He thought to himself, "Well, this must be it. This must be what it is like to be dead or at least to be on the next part of the journey." And, as there was nothing else to do, he carried on walking along the road.

They walked a very long way and the man was becoming hot and tired when he came to a fork in the road. One of the forks carried on and looked very much like the road he had journeyed on so far. The other fork was paved with golden cobblestones and it led up a hill. At the top was an arch made of marble. He walked up the hill to the arch and saw that there were gates closed before him. They were made of the finest mother of pearl. A man in a suit suddenly appeared as if from nowhere. He said, "Sir, you are most welcome here."

The man with the dog replied, "But where am I?"

"Sir, you are in Heaven and we have been waiting for you."

"Oh my goodness, I don't know what to say. Except that, well, I am glad to be here. But please, I have travelled a very long way. Would you have a glass of water?"

The gates then swung open and a little cherub flew down, flapping his little wings and holding a glass of the most refreshing looking water.

"Thank you," said the man, "and could I also have a drink for my dog?"

Suddenly, the man in the suit stepped in front of him, barring his way. He said "I'm sorry, Sir, but we can't allow pets in here."

The man looked at his dog then turned back and thanked the man. He said, "Well, I guess that this isn't the place for me." The man and his dog then walked back down the road and took the other fork and carried on, on their journey.

Eventually, they came to another fork. Again, one fork carried on much the same as the road they had been on. But the other fork was a dirty, dusty old track that led up to a hill that was covered in trees. They went up to the top where there was an old gate that had never been closed in a long, long time. Through the gate they saw a man leaning against a tree, sitting peacefully.

"Excuse me, would you have a drink of water?"

"Sure," said the man under the tree, "there is a water pump right over there. Come in and help yourself." Before the man entered he said, "How about a drink for my dog too?"

"Well, there should be a bowl by the pump."

They went straight to the pump and both drank the clear, cold water until they felt refreshed. They both felt an awful lot better.

"What do you call this place?" the traveller asked.

The man under the tree replied, "This is heaven."

"But there was a place down the road that was called heaven too."

"You mean the place with the pearly gates?" The man smiled and shook his head, "That's not heaven. That's hell."

"Well, that's very strange. Doesn't it annoy you that they call it heaven?"

"Well no, not really. We are just glad they are able to take all the people who would leave their friends behind.

A version of this story was told by the American storyteller, Dan Keding and it also found its way onto an unattributed mass-circulated email, a modern way of circulating stories. The story, which can be told with either a woman or man as the central figure, is about friendship and particularly the ideals of loyalty and sacrifice in friendship. The quality of friendship is important to explore with children – what makes a good friend? Are friends important? What is it like to argue with a friend? – and there are many stories that offer the opportunity to do this in looking at how characters might treat each other which offer the opportunity to reflect on friendship.

Maybe

Once, there was a farmer who lived in the north of China. He lived with his father and some would say he was a rich young farmer and they would also say that because he had one horse, and not many farmers had a horse, he was well off indeed.

Now, one day his horse ran away over the border to the land of the nomads. Everybody in the village came to offer him comfort and sympathised with him, agreeing with him when he said, "This is a catastrophe."

The farmer went to tell his father and he said, "Father, I have lost my horse. This is a disaster. It is a catastrophe."

Now the old man, who had been around a long time, had seen a thing or two, and knew the ways of the world well, said, "You say it is a catastrophe. Well maybe it is or maybe it isn't. How can you tell? What makes you so sure? How do you know that this is not a blessing?"

Well, one week later, the horse returned and it had brought with him a beautiful stallion, one of the most wonderful horses that the nomads used to keep. The farmer was delighted and all his neighbours came to congratulate him and agreed with him, "This, indeed, is a great blessing."

The son went to tell his father, but the father just said, "You say this is a blessing. Well maybe it is or maybe it isn't. How can you tell? What makes you so sure? How do you know that this is not a catastrophe?"

The son paid no attention to his father who just seemed to want to unsettle him. He was now even richer and he would spend his days riding the beautiful creature. But the horse was wild, and one day, it bucked and threw the farmer up into the air. He landed badly and broke his hip, he became lame. Everyone came to console the farmer and to offer sympathy. When the farmer told his father it was a catastrophe, the father just said, "Maybe it is, maybe it isn't. How do you know that this is not a blessing?" Well, how do you think the son felt about that?

Now, this story has two endings so you can choose which one you like best.

Not long after the fall, the nomads came from across the border and invaded the country. The people of the land had to fight back and the King had to raise an army. Everybody had to fight but things did not look good. Nine out of ten of the people who went to fight the nomads died in the war.

One day the conscription officers came to take everyone in the farmer's village and to put them in the army. They took everyone but when they saw the farmer they took one look at him and they said, "You Sir, are lame, you cannot fight. You stay in the village. Go and look after your father." So it was the son went to live with his father and they looked after each other till the end of their days. They lived happily and meditated long on the way of the world, that what can seem like disasters can turn into great things and what can seem like triumphs can turn into disasters. Things will always change and change is the only thing that is constant. It is the great mystery of the world that cannot be understood, only accepted.

Now, the other ending.

Well, the nomads invaded and the soldiers came to the village to get people to fight. They looked at the farmer and they said, "You can't fight. You're lame. Go and live with your father." The villagers all congratulated the farmer on his good fortune. He would live and they would surely die. The farmer went to tell his father the good news and the father said, "You think this is good news. Well, maybe it is and maybe it isn't." And so it goes on, for this story is without end.

Contained in this story is an insight about the ever-changing nature of things and that events are not always what they seem. Originally a Taoist parable, this version is based on two sources; Jane Yolen's 'Favourite Folk Tales from Around the World' and from 'Reframing' by John Bandler and Richard Grindler.

The Greatest Gift

There once were three brothers, Tom, Sam and Jack. They had a favourite uncle who travelled a lot. He promised that everywhere he went he would bring one of them a present. His next trip was to China, where science was far more developed than at home. From China, the uncle brought Tom a spyglass (or telescope). This spyglass had special powers. When Tom looked through it, he could see things happening thousands of miles away on the other side of the globe. Sam and Jack wondered what on earth their presents could be.

The uncle's next journey was to Persia. From this trip he brought Sam a richly coloured rug. However, this carpet also had special powers. If anyone sat on it and said the magic words, the carpet would become airborne and propel the riders to wherever they desired to go. Jack was breathless with anticipation as to what his present would be.

The uncle's last trip was to Spain. From Spain he brought Jack back a lemon. At first Jack was hugely disappointed, for after all, hadn't his brothers got a magic spyglass and a flying carpet? However, the uncle explained that the lemon had curative powers, and slices of it could heal a sick person.

That very day, Tom peered through his spyglass and, on the other side of the world, saw the castle of a rich man. The rich man's daughter was confined to bed; she was as white as the pillow she was lying on. In short, she was dying. Her father, in desperation, proclaimed that if anyone could save his beloved daughter's life they would receive a bag of gold and the daughter's hand in marriage.

Tom shouted to his brothers that they must go and help the lass. Sam got them all to sit firmly on his carpet. The three brothers uttered the magic words and the carpet slowly lifted into the air. In no time at all they were flying above the clouds and to the south. Whilst Tom and Sam gripped the edge of the carpet, Jack clung on to the lemon. After an exciting but thankfully uneventful flight of some hours, the carpet drifted slowly to the ground beside the rich man's castle.

Was the rich man pleased to see them? He was not! He stormed out to the three surprised brothers. "As if things weren't bad enough, I've got my beloved daughter at death's door and you three turn up!"

The brothers protested that they had come to save the daughter's life, and insisted on being taken to her room. She looked up from her pillow. Was she pleased to see them? She was not! "As if I wasn't feeling bad enough – boys! Push off!" The brothers protested that they had come to help her. Jack cut a slice of his lemon and placed it in her mouth. Almost immediately some colour returned to her cheeks and a smile spread across her face. Encouraged, Jack cut another slice of lemon, placing it in her mouth followed by another and another. By now the lass had miraculously jumped out of bed and was dancing round the room to peals of laughter. The father was so delighted by his daughter's recovery that he presented the three brothers with the bag of gold to share between them. However, he had a problem. Only one of the three could receive the reward of her hand in marriage.

This is the dilemma. Who should marry the daughter? Should it be Tom, Sam or Jack?

This is another story from American storyteller, Dan Keding, who told this old Croatian story. Some themes arising in this story are being given unequal gifts and the benefits of working together. The end of the story presents a dilemma that may be the starting point of a debate. Facilitative questions might include; Who should receive the reward of the daughter's hand in marriage? Should it be Tom, for without his spyglass they would never have known that the lass was dying? Should it be Sam, for without his magic carpet they would never have been able to travel to help? Or should it be Jack, for without the curative powers of his lemon she would not have recovered? Is it possible to decide between the gifts?

Of course the person who gave the greatest gift and therefore most deserved the reward was Jack. Tom still has his spyglass; Sam still has his magic carpet, but Jack gave away the only thing he had to help someone in need. However, students might want to reach their own conclusions about who deserves the reward and whether it would be a valued or desired reward. An older version of this story is contained in 'The Arabian Nights' called the Three Princes and the Princess Nouronihar' that might be suitable for adolescents. Here, there is no difference between the gifts, the fruit does not lose its power through being smelt but there is some attraction between the bearer of the fruit and the girl. Another version of the story is found in Turkey, which goes to show that 'stories have legs'.

The Ring of Solomon

The great King Solomon was said to be the wisest of kings and this story is about how he gained that wisdom. Solomon had a faithful servant who he could always rely upon to do whatever he asked. Now, it was the way of Solomon to leave his great palace and to disguise himself and walk amongst his people so he knew what they were thinking and what their concerns and worries were, so he knew the voice of the people.

One day, he saw his servant who was talking to a group of people and he was boasting about his relationship with the King. He was saying, "Whenever Solomon wants something done, he always comes to me because he knows I will always be able to do whatever he asks."

Solomon thought that he needed to teach his servant some humility, to not think so much of himself. He thought of a task that he would set his servant that he knew could not be achieved, perhaps then the servant would not be so boastful. The King called his servant to him and said, "I wish you to find me a ring that can make a sad man happy and a happy man sad. I will give you one year and one day and then you must bring it to me."

"I will do that thing for you," said the servant and he set off. At first the servant was full of enthusiasm for his task and he went to every jeweller's in every bazaar and market and he would ask, "Would you have a ring that would make a happy man sad and a sad man happy?" But each time there was always the same reply, "There is no such thing."

The man travelled many miles over deserts and over mountains to new and strange countries but he could still not find what he was looking for. The time at last came when he had to return to Solomon. One year and one day later he arrived back at the marvellous palace of Solomon. Outside the palace there was a small market. The man, desperate by now, thought it was worth one last chance and he looked amongst the stalls in the market. Right at the very edge of the market he saw a small boy who had a cloth spread out on the ground. On the cloth were a few trinkets and among them there were some rings. Could it be that he might find what he was looking for here? He went up to the boy and said, "Would you have a ring that would make a sad man happy and happy man sad?"

The boy looked long and hard at him and finally said, "Don't be stupid. There is no such thing".

At that the man turned round and headed towards the palace. You could tell by his walk that he was defeated. Each step he made was heavy and his shoulders were stooped as he knew he had failed in his task. But the boy's grandfather had been watching this from a distance and as the servant walked by he called over to him.

"What is it that you are looking for?" the old man asked.

The servant said, "I am looking for a ring that would make a sad man happy and a happy man sad, but I now know there is no such thing."

The man called to the boy, "Bring me that ring that is at the centre of the blanket." The boy brought it over. It was a plain old ring made of iron and starting to rust. The old man took it and engraved some words in the finest of writing on the ring and passed it to the servant. As the servant read the words on the ring a huge smile spread across his face. He asked the man how much he wanted for the ring, but the old man said that he could have it for free as he had surely looked for it for long enough. The servant thanked the man, turned and walked towards the palace with a spring in his step.

Now the palace of Solomon was one of the great wonders of the world. It was a magnificent building filled with the most unbelievable treasures and works of art. It also contained many rare and important books and the finest minds of the land were drawn there. In the centre was Solomon's throne and its owner was waiting there for his servant to return. He had a wry smile across his face as he thought how humble his servant would now have to be. "I know he will feel that he has let me down, so I must break it to him gently that I had set him a task that he could not possibly succeed in," thought Solomon, "and this was to help him learn some humility." But then he saw his servant enter the grand room and his walk showed not the slightest trace of despair. He walked up to the King and he handed his master the ring. Solomon took the ring and looked at it carefully. He read the words engraved upon it. And the smile that was on his face fell as he read the words, "This too shall pass." He looked round him at the beauty and splendour of his court and he realised that all of this would be as dust one day. All that he had created would be as nothing. He looked at his servant again and he realised his servant had indeed done what he had been asked as this ring would make a happy man sad and a sad man happy. A happy man would be reminded that his happiness would pass away and a sad man would remember that his time of sadness too would pass.

Solomon thanked his servant and took from his own finger the most ornate and precious ring he had and gave it to his servant. He took the old plain iron ring and placed it on his own finger where it stayed until the end of his days and was there as a constant reminder to him of the transience of all things.

This old Jewish tale, of which another printed version can be found in Heather Forest's collection of Wisdom Tales, again speaks of the intransigence of things. It also reflects an emotional truth also, that strong feelings will also peak and pass.

The Spirit in the Bottle

There was once a Woodcutter who was very poor and he spent his days chopping wood from dawn until dusk. Now this Woodcutter had a son, and he decided that he did not want his son to spend his days chopping wood as he did and he wanted him to get on in the world. Also, if he did get on in the world he might be able to look after his old father who wouldn't have to chop wood day in and day out anymore. So every day the Woodcutter worked an extra hour to be able to put aside a little bit of money to send his son off to get an education. When the boy was old enough he went away to college where he worked hard and was well liked. But the money did what the money always does, it ran out. The boy had to return home and when he did so his father was not pleased.

"What am I going to do with you now?" he said to his son.

"Well," said the boy, "I could come out and chop wood with you."

"You! Look at you. Your head is full of books and you are not fit to do a full day's work," said the Woodcutter.

"Give me a chance," said the boy, "I can prove that I can do it."

"Well, even if you could, you have not got an axe that you could use," said the father.

And so it carried on but the boy persisted and eventually the father went and borrowed an axe from a neighbour and the next day they both set out to the forest. They began chopping wood early in the morning and carried on till the sun was high in the sky. At that point the Woodcutter said to the boy, "Stop chopping now. It is time for us to rest".

But the boy was fascinated just to be in the forest. It was a beautiful magical place. He said, "I want to explore this beautiful place."

But his father just replied, "Don't be a fool. You need to save your strength for this afternoon's work. You must stop now."

But the boy could not rest. He was too curious and he started to explore the forest. The rays of the sun shone through the leaves to create the most beautiful patterns, everywhere he looked, he saw the most wondrous things. He explored deep into the forest until he arrived at the very heart and there he saw a tree. This was no ordinary tree. It was the biggest tree he'd ever seen. If six men stood in a circle with their arms outstretched and their fingers just touching, then that would just be the span of this tree. As he looked up in wonder, he heard a little voice saying, "Let me out." He looked around and heard it again, "Let me out. Let me out." It seemed to be coming from the ground and he searched through the fallen leaves. He found a small bottle just a few inches tall with a cork in the top. Inside the bottle was a little man.

The young man pulled the cork stopper out of the bottle and as soon as he did so the little man disappeared and the bottle was full of the most dense smoke. The smoke began to come out of the bottle and soon began to spiral round like a tornado, faster and faster and higher and higher. Soon it reached almost to the top of the tree and suddenly it disappeared. In its place was a huge spirit who looked down at the boy.

"You have released me from the prison where I have been kept for fifteen hundred years. And do you know what your reward shall be?" bellowed the Spirit.

"No, I don't," said the boy although he had heard stories that there were often wonderful rewards when such spirits as these were set free from their bottles.

"Your reward shall be that I will pick you up and twist you until your neck is broken."

"Why would you do such a thing? I thought I would get some reward for setting you free. I haven't hurt you!" proclaimed the boy.

"I have waited a long time in this bottle. When I was first imprisoned I would have loved and served whosoever set me free. But no one came. I waited and grew angry. Then I swore that I would kill the first person that I would meet. And that is you."

The boy had to start thinking quickly. He said to the Genie, "Well if I have to die then it must be so, but I'd much rather it was at the hands of an honest man than someone like you."

"What? Are you calling me a liar?" said the spirit. "I can assure you I am honest and your death will be honest too."

"I don't believe you," said the boy, "you told me that I released you from this tiny little bottle. Look at the size of you. You could never have a fit in such a tiny thing. You are trying to trick me."

"Oh, it was me alright," said the spirit.

"Prove it!" said the boy.

"So I shall," and the spirit instantly transformed back into a whirling spiral of smoke that sucked itself back inside the bottle. As soon as all the smoke was inside the young man put his thumb over the top of the bottle. He picked up the cork and screwed it back in tight. Inside the smoke changed back into the little man and he was trapped again.

"Let me out," said the little man. "Let me out and I will give you a most extraordinary reward."

Well, what would you do in that situation? The boy had almost lost his life, but he had managed to get the spirit back in the bottle. So, maybe he thought it was worth the chance to gain something wonderful. He unscrewed the cork. Again the little man turned to smoke and poured out of the bottle and turned again into a great spirit.

The boy looked at him. He was trembling but he managed to say, "Well, what is my reward?"

The spirit twisted his hand and in it appeared a cloth. He said, "If you were to rub any wound with this side of the cloth it will instantly be healed. If you rub any metal with the other side of the cloth, it will turn the basest of metals into silver."

The boy took the cloth from the spirit and went over to a tree. He took out his axe and smashed it into the tree causing a piece of bark to splinter off. He placed the bark back against the tree and rubbed it with his cloth. Immediately, the cut disappeared and the tree's wound was healed. The boy went back to the spirit and thanked him. The spirit bowed low and then turned and disappeared.

The boy returned to his father. When the Woodcutter saw him, he was furious. "Where have you been? Don't you know you have work to do," he shouted. The boy went straight to work and he picked up his axe. As he did so the axe head rubbed against the cloth that the spirit had given him. He struck the axe against the tree, but as the axe head was now made of silver and being a soft metal, it bent. The Woodcutter could not see that the metal had turned to silver, but he could see that the axe was now bent and useless. "Look at what you've done. Now I will have to pay for this axe as well. Bringing you with me has been a complete waste of time," said the Woodcutter bitterly.

"Father, let us go home," said the boy, but the Woodcutter just kept on complaining about how much money the boy was costing him. Eventually the boy persuaded him and they both returned to the village.

"Father, how much is this axe worth?" said the boy.

"It will cost at least 12 shillings. That is money that I do not have," said the Woodcutter. "Do not worry," said the boy and he went off to the metal-smith and asked him how much the lump of silver was worth.

"This is worth much more than I have to give you," said the metal-smith. The young man took what the metal-smith could give him and he told his father exactly what had happened in the forest. The neighbour who had lent the axe was repaid and the Woodcutter never had to work a day in his life again. And the boy could now afford to return to his studies and it is said that he went on to become the greatest doctor in the entire world.

This story was recorded by the Brothers Grimm in their famous collection of folk stories. The story is what Michael Meade, in his book 'Men and the Water of Life', describes as an initiatory story. Such stories are about the transition from child to adult and are a common theme in traditional tales. As such, these stories can assist in the initiation in to adulthood and are particularly useful to adolescent boys who are often engaged in the developmental task of working out what kind of man they wish to become. In this story, the young boy who has not completed an education faces the shame of the father, but the boy is persistent to succeed. His enthusiasm for life takes him to the heart of the forest where he overcomes the destructive force of the spirit angry at being imprisoned for so long. In so doing he attains his manhood and liberates his father and is able to complete his education through his own resources. The question may be what is it that the spirit in this story represents? Is it so powerful that it must be imprisoned or transformed?

The Sheep Thieves

There were two brothers who lived high in the hills in a sheep farming country. These brothers were idle and dishonest; not for them the sweat of the land! They waited for dark, foggy nights and slunk out to steal sheep.

The local farmers soon tired of this. The villains had to be taught a lesson. The farmers instructed the village blacksmith to fashion a branding iron with the letters 'ST' for 'Sheep Thief'.

The next dark, foggy night, two of the toughest farmers went out and caught the brothers at their wicked work. They forced their arms up behind their backs, marched them to the forge and strapped them to chairs. The branding iron was heated to red heat. Even though the brothers pleaded for mercy the hot iron was pressed to their foreheads. There were screams of agony and the smell of burning flesh as each thief had the letters 'ST' branded on their forehead.

The youngest brother decided to make a fresh start. He left the hills for the flatlands and landed up in a village. As is the way in villages, the locals wondered about the incomer. In particular, the locals mused on the letters 'ST'. In their wisdom, the villagers presumed the 'ST' was short for 'Saint'. They were so proud to have a saint arrive in their village that they gave him a cottage to live in, food to eat, and employment. Because it is the way with most people most of the time that they behave in a way that is expected of them, he no longer felt the need to steal. In fact when this man died in the village, beyond his three score years and ten, he was buried in the village churchyard a saint, and indeed had become a saint.

The older brother, high in the hills, was branded a sheep thief and treated like a sheep thief. Because it is the way with most people, most of the time that they behave in a way that is expected of them, he continued to be a thief. Well before his three score years and ten, he was caught stealing sheep, brought before the justice and sentenced to be hanged by the neck until dead.

The twelve-year-old Dorset girl who told Taffy this story assured him the man was the last in England ever to be hanged for stealing a sheep. The story points to the way that people will behave according to the role that they are cast in. So it might be preferable to cast people into positive roles and resist from more negatives ones. As Goethe said, "Treat people as if they were what they ought to be, and you help them to become what they are capable of being."

Co-operation

Many years ago, in a remote village in Africa a young man proudly took his intended to meet his father. He told his father this was the woman he wished to marry. The father asked the young girl if she was sure she wanted to marry his son. The father told the son that before he could agree to the marriage the young man had a test to pass. He asked the son to walk across the yard and pick up an enormous lump of rockstone and carry it back to him. The young man flexed his muscles and grasped the boulder. No matter how hard he tried he was unable to lift the rock. His father tutted in derision. He asked the woman if she really was interested in being married to a man who was so weak. He pointed out that if enemies raided their village he might not be strong enough to protect his wife and children. The young woman believed this, turned her back on the young man and walked off down the road. The young man was both angry and upset, and immediately started a programme of exercise to build up his muscles.

Some months later the young man again brought a woman to meet his father, announcing this was the woman he wanted to marry. Again the father asked the woman if this was what she desired, then reminded the son of the test he would have to pass before the marriage could be agreed. Feeling a little more confident, the young man approached the rockstone. He grasped the stone and managed to lift it off the ground. However, he was still not strong enough to carry it over to his father, and let it fall. Again the father in derision asked the young woman if she really wanted someone that weak as her husband. The young woman turned her back on the young man and his father and walked off down the road. This time the son was even more angry and distraught.

Six months later the son brought a new woman to meet his father. The father again explained the task to both his son and his intended. The son strode towards the enormous stone and grasped it. When the young woman saw him struggling with the rock, she walked over and grabbed the other side of it. Together they carried the rock and placed it at the father's feet. The father smiled, and looking his son in the eye, said, "This is the woman you should marry, for marriage is about working together, if you do not do that then it will be very hard work for both of you and if you do then it will all be much easier." He gave his permission for the wedding to take place. As far as I know, the two lived together, co-operating with each other for the rest of their days.

This story from the Caribbean was told by storyteller Winston Nzinga who also performs under the name of Yam. A powerful teaching story that marriage is about working together and that message is amplified through being given as an unexpected twist at the end of the tale.

The Search for Happiness

There was once a man who had everything money could buy, but was still unable to find happiness. One morning, he decided to journey to find happiness. He put on his ankle-length sheepskin coat, mounted his horse and set off down the road. A little into his journey, he rounded a bend and met a peasant woman weeping beside a dead horse. Her eyes were dulled with despair - almost lifeless - and lines of stress and trouble were etched into her forehead. He asked the woman why she was in such distress and she told him that with this horse dead she would be unable to plough her land, or travel the distance to market, and would therefore probably die of starvation. The traveller dismounted his horse and gave it to the poor woman as a gift. As he did this, the sparkle came back into her eyes, and the carelines fell from her brow and her cheeks. The traveller thought, "How strange that so little could make someone happy". He continued on his journey on foot.

The farther he travelled, the thicker the dust in his hair and beard, and on his boots. His eyes became dulled with the exhaustion and loneliness of travelling. His journey took him up a mountain. At the top of the mountain he found a naked man shaking with the cold behind a rock. His eyes were dulled and his face a mask of terror, as he was on the brink of death from hypothermia. The traveller removed his sheepskin coat and, placing it around the shoulders of the shivering man, he hugged him so that the warmth from his own body could pass to the old man, dragging him back from the brink of death. As the old man recovered a little, his eyes began to sparkle and a smile spread across his face. The traveller thought, "How strange that so little should make someone happy", and continued on his own journey to find happiness.

The farther he travelled, the thicker the dust in his hair and beard, and on his boots. His eyes became dulled with the exhaustion and loneliness of travelling. Descending the mountain, the traveller came to an encampment where a starving family were huddled around a fire, their faces were racked with hunger and their eyes dulled with the desperation that starvation brings. Reaching into his shoulder bag, the traveller took out a hunk of bread and a piece of fruit – all he had - and gave it to the parents and their three children, who shared it out. As they swallowed the first food they had had for many days, their eyes began to sparkle and smiles wreathed their faces. The traveller thought, "How strange that so little should make someone happy," and continued on his own journey to find happiness.

The farther he travelled, the thicker the dust in his hair and beard, and on his boots. His eyes became dulled with the exhaustion and loneliness of travelling. The traveller walked into a village. In the middle of the village a group of women were washing clothes in a stream. The traveller noticed one very slight, shy young woman who, realising she was being looked at or even admired, bolted down the lane into her cottage. The traveller noticed where she had gone and, plucking up courage went and knocked on the door. The woman came out and looked into the dullness and exhaustion of his eyes. Without a word, she put her arms around his shoulders and gave him a hug. As she did so, the dust fell from his beard, his eyes began to sparkle, and a smile came to his lips. The woman thought, "How strange that so little could make someone happy".

Singer, songwriter and storyteller Rory McLeod told this story to Taffy. It is reminiscent of the proverb; 'It is impossible to do good to others without doing good for oneself.'

The King of the Birds

The birds of the air were discussing which should be the king of the birds. In this situation, it is quite usual that someone steps forward as self-appointed leader! So it was that the golden eagle decided he was the biggest and best and strutted around boasting and bragging: "Me, I'm the biggest, I'm the best." The trouble was he became too big for his beak and the other birds tired of his boasting and posing. The chattering magpies sought the assistance of the wise old owl. They asked if the owl could devise a plan to bring the eagle down a perch or two.

The owl decided that the following day there should be a competition to see which bird could fly the highest. Hearing of this, the eagle bragged even more. He mocked the competition as a waste of time for he was biggest and best and could fly the highest.

The following day, all the birds lined up on a nearby ridge. At one end of the line was the hawk posse - the kestrel, the sparrowhawk, the osprey and, of course, the golden eagle. Next to the hawks, the big black birds fell into line – the rook, the raven, the jackdaw and the crow. Next to them, the blackbird and thrush and - of course - the chattering magpies. A colourful line of robins, bluetits and finches placed themselves between the blackbirds and an enormous line of sparrows. At the far end of the line was the smallest of all - little Jenny Wren. No sooner had they lined up than the eagle started strutting around and boasting, deriding the competition as a waste of time. The owl decided to step in. Moving along the line, he whispered something in the ear of little Jenny Wren - a cunning plan. Nodding, she tiptoed around the back of the line. The eagle was so busy boasting and posing, he didn't notice as the wren climbed onto his back and nuzzled down in the feathers.

The owl took three steps backwards and pronounced, "On your marks . . . get set . . . GO". The sky was black with birds. The sparrows were the first to tire and drifted down to land. Soon after, the coloured birds – the robins, bluetits and finches - became weary and landed. Even the magpies, the thrush, the blackbird and the big black birds – the rook, the raven, the jackdaw and the crow – wearied and glided back to earth. Yet high in the sky the hawks had found a thermal and continued to soar. Eventually, even they tired and the kestrel, sparrowhawk and osprey gracefully glided down, leaving one speck high in the sky, the speck that was the golden eagle.

The hawks commented that although the eagle had been boastful, he had merely told the truth, as he was the strongest and had flown the highest. No sooner had the hawks decided this than the eagle began to tire and commenced his descent. On his back, little Jenny Wren felt the change in altitude and launched herself upwards. Just for this moment, the eagle was coming down while the wren still climbed upwards. On landing the eagle of course continued to boast that the competition had been a waste of time as he had proved himself the biggest and best. The other birds pointed to the tiniest speck still high in the sky - the speck that was Little Wren. Drifting down, the wren was encircled by all the rest of the birds, who pointed out that she was the King of the Birds for although she was the smallest in size, she was the biggest in wit.

The wren, the wren, is King of the Birds
Saint Stephen's Day she was stuck in the furze
Although she was little, her wit it was great
If you boast like an eagle, you may yet share his fate!

The Snipe

A hunter, a man with a gun, was walking up a hill. On his way he met a hen snipe, a wading bird with a long thin bill. Angrily, the mother snipe challenged him, "You nasty, cruel man. You're going up there to murder my beautiful chicks."

Defensively, the hunter promised that he wouldn't.

At the top of the hill it was BANG, BANG and BANG, as he shot everything that moved. He headed down the hill with a string of brown birds tied beak-to-tail. Again meeting the hen snipe, she burst into tears: "As well as being cruel, you are a cheat and a liar. You promised you wouldn't kill my beautiful chicks." The hunter replied that he hadn't killed any beautiful chicks; he had just shot some plain, brown birds. The mother snipe said, "Then you are a fool as well as a cheat and a liar. Every mother thinks her young is beautiful, no matter what they look like".

The Tiger and the Four Antelopes

One morning a tiger woke up hungry and fancied a nice juicy meal of antelope meat. He travelled and located a small herd of four antelopes, and decided that one of those would be his meal for the day. He then realised the antelopes had sharp teeth, pointy horns and heavy hooves. In short, they could bite him, prong him and kick him to death. The tiger decided discretion was the better idea. He lay and waited until one antelope moved a hundred metres from the herd. The tiger decided this would be his victim. However, with only a hundred metres between the lone antelope and his herd, the other three could still race over to kick, bite and prong. The tiger had to come up with a plan to further separate his victim. He crept up to the one on his own, but passing close enough to the other three to pretend to listen to them. He asked the lone antelope whether the other three were its friends. The lone antelope said they were very good friends. The tiger stated that this was not so, as when he passed the group of three, they had been talking about the other one, saying it was fat and ugly. The lone antelope said that in that case, it would have nothing to do with the others ever again, and moved a further hundred metres away from the herd. It was now fair game. The tiger sprinted up, pounced, killed and pulled the antelope limb from limb, gorging on the flesh. Having eaten so much meat, the tiger felt sleepy. Nodding off to sleep, the tiger realised that if he again woke up hungry, he could locate the antelopes again, as there were still three remaining.

Some time later, the tiger woke up hungry. He went and found the 'Gang of Three', but realised they too had sharp teeth, sharp pointy horns and heavy hooves. He lay and waited until one moved just a hundred metres from the herd. For his own safety the tiger decided to employ the same tactic: he approached the lone antelope whilst passing very close to the other two, so as to appear to be listening to them. The tiger asked the solitary antelope if the three were friends. The antelope replied that they were, but that there used to be four, but one hadn't come home the previous night. The tiger licked the dried blood from his whiskers and said innocently that he wondered what had happened to that one. Then the tiger surprised the antelope by saying that actually they weren't friends, as he had just heard the other two saying he was too old to keep up with the herd, and they were thinking of finding a new antelope - younger and trendier - to be in their herd. The antelope said that if that were the case he would have nothing to do with them ever again, and he moved another hundred metres from the herd. He was now fair game. The tiger sprinted over, pounced, killed and gorged itself on the flesh of the antelope. Having eaten all this meat, the tiger felt sleepy, but realised that if it woke up hungry again, it could still find the remaining two antelopes.

So it was that later the tiger woke up hungry and located the two surviving antelopes, but was faced with a problem; they too had sharp teeth, pointy horns and heavy hooves, and if he was caught between them they could bite, prong and kick him to death. He needed to come up with a cunning plan to separate them, but he couldn't say that one was talking about the other because there were only the two of them left. Becoming even more devious, the tiger crept round behind one of the antelope and nipped his backside. The antelope jumped, "Who did that?" By then the tiger had crept round behind the other antelope and nipped that one's bottom. This one also jumped, "Who did that?" The tiger had slid away a safe distance, so the antelope blamed each other, locked horns and started to battle. As they tired of this, they separated, one walking off a hundred metres in one direction, and one a hundred metres in the other. They were now both fair game. The tiger picked the weakest, pounced, killed and gorged himself on the flesh and blood. Again, feeling, sleepy, the tiger nodded off, knowing that when he woke up hungry, there was still one antelope remaining on his own that he could eat whenever he wanted, and that is exactly what the tiger did.

The unity of the group of antelope is broken by the gossip of the tiger and that leads to separation. The story makes the point that gossip, and a tendency to believe it without checking it out, can destroy unity and trust and lead to vulnerability. Gossip should not be readily believed.

The Smuggler

Nasredin was a very clever smuggler. Each day he led a donkey that carried two bundles of straw up the mountain to the pass that divided two lands. At the border was a customs official and he looked at the donkey's bundles with great suspicion.

"I know you have something hidden on that animal that you are trying to smuggle into this land without paying the tax on it. Whatever it is I will find it," said the official. He proceeded to pull the bundles of straw apart and he searched for a very long time without finding anything but straw. After over an hour of looking he had to give up. At last he said, "I know you're hiding something. You are indeed a crafty smuggler but I have to let you go this time. But beware, one day I will catch you," and he looked on with a frown across his face as Nasredin walked across the border with his donkey.

Well, the next day Nasredin came again to the border with a donkey with two bales of straw upon his back and again the Customs Inspector searched the animal thoroughly. He looked through the straw, in the donkey's mouth, he even looked under the donkey's feet. Again, he could find nothing and again he had to let him cross the border.

Day after day Nasredin came to cross the border and the whole affair went on for years and years. Each day the Customs Inspector thoroughly searched the donkey, but he could find absolutely nothing. The Customs Inspector was obsessed and he couldn't stop thinking about how he was being fooled. He was always thinking of new places to look, "Maybe it is hidden between the hairs of his tail, or in his ears." But he never found anything and after ten years it was time for him to retire and he had to admit defeat.

Many years later, the Customs Inspector found he still kept on thinking about that clever smuggler and how he had been tricked all the time. One day he was sitting in a café having a cup of strong black coffee when he saw Nasredin walking along the street. He called out to him, "Hello, do you remember me? Let me buy you a cup of coffee." They sat down and drank together. The Customs Inspector said, "Every day you came across the border and I am sure you were smuggling something. I am retired now and I will do nothing. Please could you tell me what it was and put my mind at rest?"

Nasredin smiled and nodded his head. The Customs Inspector said, "Please, can you just tell me what it was you were smuggling across the border every day?"

"Donkeys," said Nasredin.

This is one of the many strange, sometimes funny, sometimes paradoxical Middle Eastern tales about the Mullah Nasredin, also known as the Hodja, and was adapted from the version in Heather Forest's 'Wisdom Tales from around the World.'. Nasredin was a cleric who can be both very wise and very stupid. He is a trickster, a figure who breaks natural or social laws, either for cunning or foolish reasons but often with beneficial effects. This story explores the theme of not seeing what is right before your eyes.

Gelert the Dog

There was once a great Prince, known as Llywelyn. As a reward for his bravery and courage he was given a hound by King John. Llywelyn loved his dog who was called Gelert. Whenever Llywelyn went out hunting he took Gelert with him where he would run deep into the woods and return immediately when he heard his master's horn. Whenever Llywelyn had to go away to fight he knew that Gelert would look after his family. He loved his dog as much as his own infant son.

One day he returned home and he saw Gelert running towards him. The dog's mouth was dripping with blood. His usual delight at returning home and seeing his faithful hound was disturbed – he knew something was wrong. He went inside the house following a trail of blood and went up to his son's room. There, he found the walls and the sheets of the bed covered in blood. The same blood that dripped from Gelert's fangs.

He called for his child but there was no reply and Llywelyn was filled with the most utter loathing for his once loved dog. 'You hell hound,' he cried and he lifted his sword and plunged it deep into Gelert's side. His anger had overwhelmed him and in an impulsive act he had struck.

Gelert gave a fearful howl as he fell to the floor, and as he died Llywelyn then heard the sound of someone crying. It was his infant son, wakened by Gelert's last cry. Llywelyn went straight to him, and was filled with the greatest joy that his son was still alive hidden under a mound of furs and unhurt. Beside the furs was the body of a great wolf that had clearly died in a bloody struggle.

Llywelyn realised at once his mistake. Gelert had protected his son and killed the wolf. Long did Llywelyn mourn for his dog and his pain was great. He buried him and built a great cairn of stones high over his grave so that Gelert should never be forgotten.

This is a well known story from Wales where there is a town, Beddgelert (The Grave of Gelert), in Gwynedd where the dog is supposed to be buried. It is not the true source of the story that has been traced back to Asia and Medieval Europe. The story of the Prince who killed the dog that saved his child tells of the impulsive anger that comes from jumping to conclusions.

Heaven and Hell

A famed Chinese warrior struggled to know the difference between heaven and hell. He thought that the way to find the answer would be to ask an esteemed teacher. So, he sought out a monk who everybody said was the greatest teacher in the land.

When the warrior met the monk he asked, "Oh venerable and honoured teacher, you are known as most wise and I respect you and bow before you." And this was exactly what he did. Then he said, "Oh master, please help me and tell me. Show me the nature of heaven and hell."

The monk looked at him and replied, "You are a fool and your arrogance will stop you learning anything from one such as me."

The warrior could not believe his ears. No one had ever spoken to him this way. He filled with rage and pulled out his sword. He swung it above his head and was about to slice off the monk's neck. He lunged but the monk coolly held up a finger and the warrior, whose reflexes were great, stopped, motionless, with his sword touching the monk's skin.

"That," said the Monk, "is Hell."

The warrior was confused for a moment and then realised the truth of the monk's words. He began to laugh, he put away his sword and bowed down before the monk.

"I thank you, Great Teacher, for the wisdom you have shown me," he said.

"And that," said the monk, "is Heaven."

An old Chinese teaching story, that is retold by Daniel Goleman, in 'Emotional Intelligence' reflects the Buddhist saying, 'Mind is reality. With one thought you can be in heaven, with another in hell.'

The Emperor's New Suit

There was once an Emperor that loved nothing more than the beauty of his own wardrobe. He only cared about having the most beautiful clothes to wear. Now, many powerful rulers spend their time thinking about how big their armies are or how happy the people are but this emperor cared only for what he looked like.

Two swindlers came to the very busy city where the Emperor lived. They made claims that they were, in fact, tailors and could make the most beautiful clothes that could ever be imagined. They said they could weave a cloth so fine that it can only be seen by people who are fit for their office and were not stupid.

When the Emperor heard about this he thought it would be very useful if he could have some new clothes that as well as being beautiful would also tell him if his ministers were up to the job. He called to meet with the so-called tailors straightaway. They told him that they could make the most impressive new suit of clothes for him were they to be given the materials that they needed. This included the finest woven gold and the most delicate silks of all. They rented a room and set up their looms and the materials they wanted were delivered. Should anybody have looked in the window they would have seen them hard at work but would not have seen any material in the looms but one man who was holding a big pair of scissors and seemed to be cutting the air and the other who was sewing with a needle but with no thread or garments to sew.

The Emperor wondered how his new suit of clothes was coming along. He wanted to go and see, but he suddenly thought what would happen if he couldn't see the material. He realised it might show that he, in fact, was not clever enough for his own office. He decided to send his Prime Minister who he thought was an honest man and could report to him about how his new suit was progressing.

The Prime Minister went to see the swindlers hard at work. He saw one working the loom and the other seem to be sewing, but although he could see a giant needle he could not see what was being sown.

"I . . . , I can't see anything," he said. The tailors looked at him shocked and aghast and the Prime Minister realised that he was going to be seen as stupid and not fit for his office.

"I can't see anything that could possibly compare with such a fine and beautiful garment as this," he said quickly and the two swindlers relaxed. He asked when the suit would be ready but the men told him they needed more gold and silk for it to be finished. The Prime Minister told the Emperor how well things were coming along but that the tailors needed more materials. The Emperor sent them what they had ordered, oblivious to the cost.

Later still, the Emperor sent another of his ministers to see how things were going. And again the Minister could not see a thing, but he realised that he must act as if he could. "This is the most beautiful set of clothes I have ever seen. Look at the most beautiful patterns and colours, they seem to shimmer in front of my eyes," he said to the two swindlers who were sitting in front of an empty loom. He too went back to the Emperor and as an effort to ensure that the Emperor knew that he had seen the clothes he said. "Your Majesty, these clothes are so magnificent it would be a great idea to parade them through the town so everybody could see them."

The Emperor thought this was a marvellous idea and when he heard that the clothes were ready he went to the tailors taking with him his small entourage of ministers. As soon as they entered the room all of the ministers began to say, "Oh look at these marvellous clothes," and they pointed to the empty loom. The swindlers held up their arms as if they were holding something and said "Your Majesty, here are your trousers, your coat and your new cloak." But the Emperor thought to himself, "What is this, I can't see anything at all. Am I unfit to be an Emperor?" He realised he could not do anything but to say that his clothes were the most beautiful he had ever seen. Well, everybody seemed to be delighted and the Emperor, in fact, appointed the two swindlers as his Imperial Weavers. "Your cloth has my most gracious approval," he declared.

"Now, Your Majesty," said one of the swindlers, "these clothes are as light as a cobweb and when you wear them, well, it is as if you're wearing nothing at all they are so light. Now if you care to undress we will help you put the clothes on so they do not get damaged in any way."

When the Emperor had undressed the swindlers pretended to put all the clothes on him very carefully and slowly. All the ministers carried on saying, "How beautiful they are!" and "What a lovely fit!" and "Oh, they really are magnificent." When he was ready the cloak bearers were called and they stretched their hands to the ground and pretended to pick something up for they too did not want to look like they were stupid. As the Emperor passed the mirror he turned and looked at it. He admired himself so that people should know that he could see these clothes that he was wearing.

The procession began and they walked through the town and all the people came out and many of them were clapping and cheering. Everybody seemed to try and clap and cheer louder than the person next to them for nobody wanted anybody else to know that they could not see anything. So it was that the Emperor's clothes had never been more admired than they were that day.

However, there was a young child who had not heard anything about these clothes that could not be seen by those who were stupid. And as he saw the Emperor he said loudly, "But he has nothing on at all." Somebody heard the child and he said, "Listen to the child. That is the voice of someone who sees clearly." Soon it spread amongst the people that the Emperor had nothing on at all and people began to shout out, "Look at the Emperor! He has nothing on!" Well, at last the Emperor heard this and he realised that they were indeed right, but he thought to himself, "While I am in this situation there is nothing I can do but to carry on." So he kept on walking with great dignity as did all his ministers and so did those that carried his cloak which did not exist.

This well-known but rarely told story was written by Hans Christian Andersen and may have been inspired by older folk tales. This tale is a very clear illustration of the power of belief, of seeing what you what to see and the fear of appearing stupid that becomes a self-fulfilling prophecy.

Trouble

One day a woman was walking beside a forest. Balanced on her head was a big jar of honey. She was going to market to sell the honey, and she was going to buy a new dress with the money she got for the honey. Actually, she was so busy thinking about her new dress she didn't look where she was walking. She tripped over a stick and, falling over, the jar of honey fell to the ground and smashed into a million yellow, sticky pieces. The woman was furious. She shook her fist at the heavens: "Papa God, Papa God, why do you bring me nothing but trouble? Trouble, Trouble, Trouble."

There was a monkey sitting at the top of the tree, who watched what happened and learnt a new word. Sometimes when we learn a new word, we get the meaning wrong and use it incorrectly. The monkey scrambled down the tree and hopped over the yellow, sticky splodge on the ground. He dipped his paw in it, put it to the tip of his tongue, and licked it, and liked it. He exclaimed, "If that's trouble, I like it. Where can I find some more of that trouble." The monkey scampered off.

Near the village, there was a farmer hoeing a field. The monkey stood staring. The farmer looked down at the monkey and enquired, "What are you looking for?"

The monkey answered, "I'm looking for Trouble. Trouble, Trouble, Trouble." The farmer responded that if the monkey was looking for trouble he would give him some, and chased him off his land.

The monkey ran into the village. A woman by the well was washing clothes in a bucket of water. The monkey stood staring. The woman looked down at the monkey and enquired, "What are you looking for?"

The monkey answered, "I'm looking for Trouble. Trouble, Trouble, Trouble." The woman responded that if the monkey was looking for trouble she would give him some and tipped the bucket of water over his head.

Running out of the village the monkey came to a wooden hut with a big wooden cross on one end. On the door it read, "The house of Papa God. Come in all who will." The monkey pushed open the door and tiptoed inside. Papa God was sitting in a big wooden chair at the end of the church - for that's what the building was. Papa God looked down at the monkey and enquired, "What are you looking for?"

The monkey answered, "I'm looking for Trouble. Trouble, Trouble, Trouble." Papa God announced that his job was to give people what they were looking for. Papa God put his hand behind his chair and pulled out a heavy basket. He told the monkey, "There's trouble enough for you in this basket. Take it to the middle of a desert and open it."

The monkey put the strap over his shoulder and lugged the basket to the middle of a desert. Expectantly, the monkey slowly opened the basket…. "RAAAARGH!" Out jumped three pit-bull terriers. The monkey jumped twenty metres straight up in the air. Eventually, when his paws touched the ground there was a monkey running at fifty miles an hour, chased by three pit-bull terriers. A little farther across the desert, the monkey came to a tree. Now, there's a funny thing - a tree in the middle of the desert. However, that tree was sent by Papa God to save the monkey. Papa God understands everybody has some trouble in their life, but nobody should have too much trouble. Anyway, the monkey knew that dogs can't climb trees, so he shot up to the top branch of the tree. He waited until the dogs got bored with barking at the trunk and had slunk off. The monkey scrambled back down the tree and stood with his back to the bark. He licked the last remains of the honey from the tips of his paws and said to himself: "Never trouble Trouble until Trouble troubles you".

So, the next time someone asks you what you would like on your bread or toast you can answer "Trouble". If they enquire why you call honey "Trouble", then you'll have a story to tell them, so pass it on. This story is believed to come from Africa and travelled to Jamaica through the slave trade. It was told to Taffy by storyteller Hugh Lupton.

The King's Own Storyteller

The King and the Queen had a son, the Prince. Sad it is to say, but the old king died. Every night when the boy prince went to bed his mother, the Queen, told him a story. She could teach him almost anything just through telling him a story. So it was that one night the queen decided to tackle the most difficult subject of all – mortality. She told her son that she was very old and the time was approaching when she would rejoin the king. The Prince's eyes filled with tears for he knew his mother was saying that soon she would die. Considering the consequences for himself, he said, "But if you are dead who will tell me my bedtime story?"

The Queen sadly told her son that she couldn't help with that problem, but that the day she died the boy would be crowned king. Encouraged, the boy said that if he was the King he could have anything he chose. Realising he was feeling a little stronger, the Queen agreed but warned him he would be remembered by his first decision. The boy said, "In that case my first decision will be to create a new job, the post of The King's Own Storyteller". Whoever got the job would have the task of telling him a bedtime story every night. There wouldn't be much money but it would be a pleasing job to do - for that is the way with storytelling.

One night a few months later when the Prince was still a lad, his mother the Queen peacefully died. The following day the young Prince was crowned King of the land. His courtiers enquired as to his pronouncement or decision. Confidently, the young King ordered the creation of a new job, the post of The King's Own Storyteller. The servants headed for the marketplace: "Oh Yea, Oh Yea, Oh Yea! There is a job of The King's Own Storyteller. Anyone wishing to audition for this exciting new post must come to the palace gates at 7.30 this evening". That evening there was a long queue of storytellers at the palace gates. There were men storytellers, women storytellers, fat storytellers and thin storytellers. The boy King greeted them with a cup of tea, for there is no finer way to greet a visiting storyteller. The King led them into the stateroom and made them stand around the walls. He placed a storyteller's chair in front of his throne and settled to listen to their tales. One by one the visitors sat in the hot seat and told their best story. Sadly, not one of them was good enough. The boy King thanked them and sent them home. He would have to re-advertise the post. The pronouncement went round the world that there was a new job; the post of The King's Own Storyteller. Anyone wishing to audition should queue up at the palace gates in a month's time - for it would take them that long to come from the farthest parts of the world.

A month later there was an even longer queue at the palace gates. This time there were storytellers with black skins, storytellers with red skins and feathers on their heads, storytellers with yellow skins and pigtails, even storytellers in sealskin anoraks who had made the journey in kayaks. The boy King greeted them all with a meal, for there is no finer way to greet storytellers who have travelled a long way than with a meal. The King led them into the stateroom and made them stand around the walls. He placed a storyteller's chair in front of his throne and settled to listen to their tales. One by one the visitors sat in the hot seat and told their best story. But sadly not one of them was good enough! The King thanked them and sent them off on their long journey homeward. The boy King was depressed; he hadn't had a bedtime story since the day his mother died. He decided to do the thing that many people resort to when stressed or depressed – he went for some quiet time in the garden.

As the boy King strolled into the garden with his head down and his eyes filled with tears, the old gardener was just bending to prune a rose bush. Being old, as he leaned forward, a pain shot up the gardener's spine and he let out a cry of agony: "AAAAARGH". The gardener spotted the boy King. Now the gardener knew the boy King as master and as a friend, for it was in that very garden that as a toddler, and a young Prince, he had taken his first steps and said his first word –"Grass". The gardener gently enquired, "Why are you so sad?" The boy King told his old friend that he hadn't had a bedtime story since his mother died, and couldn't find a replacement storyteller who was good enough. The old gardener thought that he had some good stories and was probably a little too old for the physical work of gardening. Nothing ventured, nothing gained, he offered the young King his services as his storyteller. Wisely, the King gratefully said that he would love the gardener to have the job, but knew he had to be seen to be fair, for he would be remembered by his first decision. Accordingly, he told the gardener that if he wanted the job, he too must come to the palace gates at 7.30 and audition the same as everyone else.

Feeling a little better, the boy King returned to the palace, knowing he would again have the company of his old friend later that day. The gardener continued to prune his roses, all the time considering which would be his best story. He decided on a story of 'Jack and the Moneylender', a moral tale some forty-five minutes long. Even whilst working, he was honing the tale. He finished work early, returned to his cottage to wash and change, for you always have to look your best when telling a story. He arrived at the palace gates in good time to be greeted by the boy King, who excitedly led him through to the stateroom. The King settled on the throne, and the gardener on the storyteller's chair, facing the King. The old man drew breath and launched into all forty-five minutes of 'Jack and the Moneylender'. At the end of the story, the boy King commended the gardener on his telling, but told him he hadn't got it quite right. However, the royal motto was 'If at first you don't succeed, try again'. He advised the gardener to return the following day, and do just that.

The gardener returned to his cottage, lit the fire and settled in his armchair to practise the story a couple more times before bed. He needed that story to be as tight as a drum skin. The following day the gardener continued to practise his tale whilst trimming the edges of his lawn. He again finished work early, and washed and changed to once more arrive at the palace in good time. Once more the boy King relaxed on the throne and the gardener in the storyteller's chair to give of his best. After three-quarters of an hour, the King told the old man that his performance was much improved but that he still hadn't got it quite right. He continued that the old adage is 'Third time lucky', and so advised the gardener to return the following day and try once more.

The gardener returned to the cottage and set a mirror in front of his armchair. He practised telling the tale in the mirror, using the reflections to devise extravagant facial expressions for the red-faced, goggle-eyed moneylender, to enrich his performance. The following day the gardener worked in the greenhouse pricking out seedlings. From time to time he glanced upwards using the greenhouse reflections to again practise his telling. With fingers crossed, and quiet confidence, he again washed and changed and made his way to the palace. The boy King wished him luck, and again settled on the throne. With some trepidation, the gardener embarked on his story. Fifteen minutes into his story the boy King's head was nodding; thirty minutes into his story, the boy King's eyes were closed. As the story concluded, after forty-five minutes, the boy King was sound asleep. The gardener tiptoed out of the room and home to his cottage. As he walked through the garden he feared the worst. He thought that he had lost the job and - even worse - perhaps his life, for the punishment in those days for upsetting the King was to have your head chopped off. Feeling desperate, the gardener went to bed and tried to find sleep.

In the middle of the night there was a thumping on the cottage door. Fearing the worst, the gardener leapt out of bed, put on his boots and clattered down the stairs. Opening the door he found two soldiers and a courtier, who announced that the King demanded his presence immediately. The gardener rubbed his neck sadly, dreading the executioner's blade. He was marched to the palace and straight to the stateroom. The boy King was still asleep on the throne in exactly the same position. Even though sound asleep we sometimes wake when a person nears our presence. So the boy King opened his eyes and greeted his old friend, "Gardener, I have some great news for you, you will be the King's Own Storyteller – the job is yours! Surprised, the gardener commented that when he had told his best story the King had gone to sleep. Even more surprisingly, the King agreed. "Yes, Gardener, you see you told the story exactly as my mother used to tell it - and that is why the job is yours".

Perhaps, in the end, if all a story does is enable you to go to sleep, to let go of the world of endless thought and cross the threshold into the restorative domain of sleep, then that is enough.

Appendices

Useful Organisations

Story Telling

Many of the organisations below will be able to provide more information about storytelling and be able to provide training

Society for Storytelling
> P.O. Box 2344,
> Reading,
> RG6 7FG
> **www.sfs.org.uk**

The Society for Storytelling is an extremely useful resource for storytelling including finding local storytelling groups that meet all over the country to share stories.

The Northern Centre for Storytelling in Lakeland
Church Stile Studio
Grasmere
Cumbria LA22 9SW
www.taffythomas.co.uk

Taffy's centre for storytelling is located in the beautiful Lake District and also has the Storyteller's Garden attached to the Centre.

Scottish Storytelling Centre
> 43-45 High Street
> Edinburgh
> EH1 1SR
> **www.scottishstorytellingcentre.co.uk**

Storytelling in Scotland is extremely well developed and this beautiful centre in the heart of Edinburgh is a resource for all things storytelling.

The George Ewart Evans Centre for Storytelling
> Ty Crawshay
> University Of Glamorgan
> Pontypridd CF37 1DL
> **http//storytelling.research.ac.uk**

Part of the University of Glamorgan, The George Ewart Evans Centre is both a teaching and academic department for storytelling.

The Forum for Storytelling in Wales
    PO Box 5162
    Cardiff CF5 9BH
    www.storytellingwales.org

The Forum for Storytelling in Wales is a newly established organisation to promote and develop storytelling in Wales

Storytellers of Ireland
    www.storytellersofireland.org
Founded in 2003, Storytellers in Ireland can be contacted through their website.

Emotional Literacy

Antidote – The Campaign for Emotional Literacy
    3rd Floor, Citside House
    40 Adler Street
    Aldgate East
    London E1 1EE
    www.antidote.org.uk

School of Emotional Literacy
    55 Parsonage Street
    Dursley
    Glos GL11 4BP.
    www.schoolofemotional-literacy.com

National Emotional Literacy Interest Group (NELIG)
    A web-based resource
    www.nelig.com

Recommended Books

Sources of Stories

The Virago Book of Fairy Tales, edited by Angela Carter (Virago, 1990)

Italian Folk Tales, retold by Italo Calvino (Penguin, 1980)

The Annotated Brothers Grimm, edited and with notes by Maria Tatar (Norton & Co. 2004)

Favourite Folktales from Around the World - edited by Jane Yolan (Random House 1986)

Wisdom Tales from Around the World, Heather Forest (August House, 1996)

South, North, East & West: The Oxfam Book of Children's Stories, edited by Michael Rosen (Walker Books, 1992)

Stories for Thinking, Robert Fisher (Nash Pollack Publishing, 1996)

Emotional Literacy

Emotional Literacy at the Heart of the School Ethos, Steve Killick (Sage/Lucky Duck, 2006)

Nurturing Emotional Literacy, Peter Sharp (David Fulton Publishing, 2001)

The Emotional Literacy Handbook, Antidote (David Fulton Publishers, 2003)

Achieving Emotional Literacy, Claude Steiner (Bloomsbury, 1997)

Emotional Intelligence - Why it can matter more than IQ. Daniel Goleman (Bloomsbury,1995)

Social Intelligence - The New Science of Human Relationships. Daniel Goleman (Hutchinson, 2006)

Further Reading on Storytelling and Emotional Literacy

Classroom Tales - Using Storytelling to build Emotional, Social and Academic Skills across the Primary Curriculum, Jenny Fox Eades (Jessica Kingsley Publishing, 2005)

Storymaking in Education and Therapy, Alida Gersie & Nancy King (Jessica Kingsley Publishers, 1989)

Therapeutic Storytelling - A Practical Guide to Developing Emotional Literacy in Primary Schools, Tricia Waters. (David Fulton Publishers, 2004)

The Magic of Metaphor: 77 stories for teachers, trainers & thinkers. Nick Owen (Crown House Publishing, 2001)

Stories, Emotional Growth and Therapy

Using Story Telling as a Therapeutic Tool with Children, Margot Sunderland. (Speechmark, 2000)

The Therapeutic Use of Stories, Edited by K.N. Dwivedi (Routledge, 1997).

Men and the Water of Life – Initiation and the Tempering of Men. Michael Meade (Harper,1993).

The Uses Of Enchantment – The Meaning and Importance of Fairy Tales. Bruno Bettleheim   (Penguin, 1976)

Connecting with Kids Through Stories – Using Narratives to Facilitate Attachment in Adopted Children. Denise Lacher, Todd Nichols and Joanne May (Jessica Kinsley Publishers, 2005)

Creative Storytelling with Children at Risk, Sue Jennings (Speechmark, 2004)

Interactive Storytelling: Developing inclusive stories for children and adults, Keith Parks (Speechmark, 2004)

Working with Particular Emotions

Bibliotherapy with Bereaved Children, Eileen Jones (Jessica Kingley Publishers, 2001)

Giving Sorrow Words - Managing Bereavement in Schools, Steve Killick & Stuart Lindeman (Sage/Lucky Duck Publishing, 1999)

Story-making in Bereavement: Dragons Fight in the Meadow, Alida Gersie (Jessica Kingsley Publishing, 1992).

Promoting Positive Behaviour - Activities for Preventing Bullying in Primary Schools, Jo Broadwood, Graham Langley and Helen Carmichael (Learning Design, London)

Making People Happy: The Nature of Happiness and its Origins in Childhood, Paul Martin (HarperPerennial 2006)

Learning from Wonderful Lives: Lessons from the Study of Well-being Brought to Life by the Personal Stories of Some Much Admired Individuals, Nick Baylis (Cambridge, 2005)

Life Choices: Teaching adolescents to make positive decisions about their lives, Phil Carradice (Sage/Lucky Duck Publishing, 2006)

The Bubblegum Guy, Joost Dorst (Sage/Lucky Duck Publishing 2004)

Anger Management: A Practical Guide for Teachers, Parents and Carers, Adrian Faupel, Elizabeth Herrick & Peter Sharp (David Fulton Publishers 1998)

Storytelling and Story Making

Creative Storytelling, Jack Zipes (Routledge, 1995)

Anyone Can Tell a Story - Bob Hartman's Guide to Storytelling, Bob Hartman (Lion Hudson, 2002)

Awakening the Hidden Storyteller: How to build a storytelling tradition in your family, Robin Moore (Shambhala Publications, 1991)

The Write Way - Creativity and Personal Development, Phil Carradice (Lucky Duck Publishing, 1996)

Impro for Storytellers, Keith Johnstone (Faber & Faber, 1999)

Impro: Improvisation and the Theatre, Keith Johnstone (Methuen 1981)

Answers to the Riddles

I have an eye but I cannot see - what am I? **A needle**

What is greater than God, worse than the devil? Rich men fear it but a poor man has it? Dead men eat it but if you eat it, you die – what is it?
Nothing

The more you take the more you leave behind. **Footsteps**

What is black when you buy it, red when you use it, grey when you throw it away? **Coal**

A beggar had a brother who lived in Spain but the brother had no brother, please explain. **The beggar was a woman**

A wizard had seven daughters and each daughter had a brother – how many children did the wizard have? **Eight**

I saw you where you never were, where you can never be. Yet, in that very place I saw you next to me. **Your reflection in the mirror**

Six arms have I, whole farms I can eat and a million of me can make a man – what am I? **A snowflake**

Ten pull a woollen sack over a calf hill. **Pulling on a sock**

What is the question that can never be answered?
What is it like to be dead?

If two is company and three is a crowd, what is four and five? **Nine**

Two coins make up 30p – one is not 20p – what are they?
20p & 10p - the other can be 20p.

How many times can you subtract 5 from 25?
Only once - after that you are subtracting it from 20.

I start with a T, end with T and am full of T – what am I? **A teapot**

A box without hinges, key or lid. Yet golden treasure inside is hid. **An egg**

You go in of one and come out of three. But when you are out, you're in. What am I?

A jumper

Before Mount Everest was discovered, what was the highest mountain in the world?

Mount Everest - *it was still the tallest even though it had not been discovered by anybody from the west.*

Thirty white horses on a red hill, first they champ, then they stand still.

Teeth

I have a mouth but never talk. I can run but never walk. I cry but never weep. I have a bed but never sleep. What am I?

A river

What do people make but no one can ever see?

Noise

What can you break with just one word?

Silence

What belongs to you that other people use much more than you do?

Your name

What has many holes but can hold water?

A sponge

What has a spine and wears a jacket?

A book

What is always before you but you cannot see it?

The future

What has a head, a foot and ears, but no neck and no legs?

A mountain
(you've heard of mountain-eers, haven't you?)

Two Legs put No Legs on Three Legs and went out. Four Legs came in and saw No Legs. Four Legs picked No Legs up and Two Legs came back in. Two Legs threw Three Legs at Four Legs who dropped No Legs and ran out. Two Legs put No Legs back on Three Legs. Who do the legs belong to?

**Two Legs is a person, No Legs is a fish,
Three Legs a three legged stool
and Four Legs is a cat.**

All of the stories in this book are traditional tales told for many generations. A few of the stories are inspired from written, as well as told tales, and versions of some of them (often with different names) can be found in the following books.

'Maybe' (The Lost Horse) Favourite Folktales from around the world - edited by Jane Yolan (Random House 1986) & Reframing – *Richard Bandler & John Grindler* (Real People Press, 1982)

'The Ring Of Solomon' (This Too Shall Pass) Wisdom Tales from around the World - *Heather Forest* (August House, 1996)

'The Spirit in the Bottle' The Complete Grimm's Fairy Tales (Routledge & Kegan Paul, 1975)

'The Smuggler' Wisdom Tales from around the World - *Heather Forest* (August House, 1996)

'Heaven and Hell' Emotional Intelligence – why it can matter more than IQ. *Daniel Goleman* (Bloomsbury,1995)

'The Emperor's New Suit' (The Emperor's New Clothes) The Complete Illustrated Stories of Hans Christian Andersen (Chancellor Press, 1983)

Abuse, sometimes families hurt (PSHEYC01) - by Yvonne Coppard
(Suitable for young adults and those working with children.)

Anger Management (PSHECH01) - by Carole Hargreaves
(Suitable for young adults and those working with children.)

Moving Up . . . Ready or Not (MISCFS01) - by Frances Snedden & Sue Whithorn
(Suitable for teachers of 9-11 year olds.)

Thinking Through Philosophy Book 1 (PSHEPC04) - by Paul Cleghorn
(Suitable for 7 - 9 year olds.)

Thinking Through Philosophy Book 2 (PSHEPC02) - by Paul Cleghorn
(Suitable for 8 - 10 year olds.)

Thinking Through Philosophy Book 3 (PSHEPC03) - by Paul Cleghorn
(Suitable for 9 - 11 year olds.)

Thinking Through Philosophy Book 4 (PSHEPC01) - by Paul Cleghorn
(Suitable for 10 - 12 year olds.)

Thinking About Personal and Social Development (PSHEPC05) - by Paul & Doris Cleghorn
(Suitable for 11 - 14 year olds.)

Let's Think (ASSEMSB01) - by Paul Cleghorn & Stephanie Baudet
(Assembly Book suitable for the whole Priamry age range.)

Raising Self Esteem in Children (PSHEAP02) - by AnnPreston & Andrea Hibbert
(Suitable for 6 - 11 year olds.)

Educational Printing Services Limited publish a full range of teachers' resources,
pupils' booklets and paperbacks.

Order on-line @ **www.eprint.co.uk**